# Librarians With Spines:
## Information Agitators In An Age Of Stagnation

Edited by
Yago S. Cura
Max Macias

Library of Congress Catalonging-in-Publication Data
Yago Cura and Max Macias
Librarians with Spines: Information Agitators in an Age of Stagnation
Includes bibliographical refrences and index
ISBN-10: 0-9845398-8-3 and ISBN-13: 978-0-9845398-8-8
Library of Congress Control Number:  2017937777

Copyrights

Editors: Yago Cura, Max Macias
Cover Design: Autumn Anglin
Interior Book Design: Autumn Anglin

Book Printing Stats: Georgia, Helevetia
Printed and Bound by : Createspace

Printed in the United States of America

**ISBN-10: 0-9845398-8-3**
**ISBN-13: 978-0-9845398-8-8**

# LIBRARIANS WITH SPINES

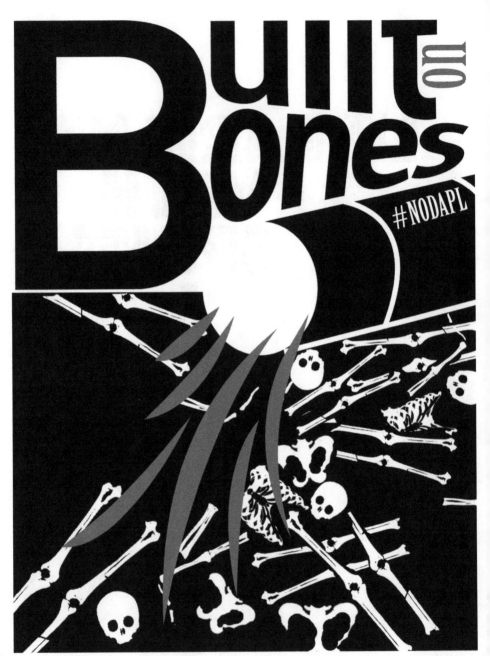

Figure 1

# Contents

# Preface

You, yes you. You deserve more of these kinds of books. You deserve to read books by authors of all stripes, creeds, and affiliations. You deserve to read books about people that have earned their spot through a praxis of hard knocks. You deserve books designed by Autumn Anglin and edited by Max Macias and Yago Cura. HINCHAS Press would like to bring you more books of this kind, would like to flood the market with books like the one in your hand.

We hope you find the chapters develop a rhythm and musicality absent from other academic texts you might have read. The book's illustrator and designer, Autumn Anglin, recommended we make Librarians with Spines a yearly series, an annual sortie per se, into the insular world of Libraries. Therefore, we hope you find inspiration enough from this volume to demand we make Librarians with Spines a yearly challenge. Please keep us honest and inquire within if you don't see something of this nature by the summer of 2018.

HINCHAS Press would like to thank Panda, Berlin, Max Macias, Autumn Anglin, James Foley, all of our insightful collaborators, the American Indian Library Association (AILA), the Asian Pacific American Librarians Association (APALA), the Black Caucus of the American Library Association (BCALA), the Chinese American Librarians Association (CALA), The National Association to Promote Library & Information Services to Latinos and the Spanish Speaking (REFORMA), LA REFORMA, the ALA Spectrum Scholars program, the Los Angeles Public Library, the

GSLIS program at Queens College/C.U.N.Y., the Vernon Branch of the LAPL, Gwendolyn Prellwitz, Sandra Ríos Balderrama, LA Futbolistas, Skateboarding, and all the people that donated to Max's GoFundMe a successful campaign.

Figure 2

# Introduction
### Yago S. Cura

*"I got 100 wild styles in my black valise"*--G.u.r.u. in Gangstarr's "B.Y.S"

In May of 2017, I get to celebrate two years of service as an Adult Librarian for the Los Angeles Public Library; I feel blessed with my position because I work with a community that benefits from resources and programming in Spanish, and I just so happen to be bilingual. Also, the branch I work at is a branch with over 100 years of service, and my purview extends to a small Black History Collection (4,208 titles). However, according to the 2011-2015 American Community Survey conducted by the United States Census, about a fifth of my patrons make less than $25,000 a year in 2017, so you can imagine the great need that exists there. In many ways, the community I service sought me out, however, I was also looking for a community to pour myself into. Likewise, Librarians with Spines exists because you have sought it out, but it also exists because it has sought you out.

Despite the fact that Max Macias (my co-editor) and I both make our living as information professionals, we are publishing this book

independent of those positions, and completely with donated funds and in-kind time donated by friends, partisans, and saboteurs. To be sure, Max and I are publishing this book as private information professional citizens, not tied to any organization nor their funds. However, the work I do as a librarian in South Central Los Angeles allows me to pay my bills, and run an online literary journal, Hinchas de Poesía (www.hinchasdepoesia.com), that I have been publishing since 2009. Again, I feel very blessed to work with an amazingly talented designer, Jennifer Therieau, and a talented editor, Jim Heavily. We don't make any money and we don't ask for any money, so a lot of people in Los Angeles do not know how to process our existence, and that's fine, as it is equally hard for us to sometimes process our own existence.

In 2016, I started HINCHAS Press after a successful campaign on Kickstarter. Our objective was to publish an anthology of ghazals written to, for, or about James Foley, the American combat journalist murdered by ISIS in 2014. Foley reported alongside the Indiana National Guard in Afghanistan and Iraq, suffered through 44 days of captivity reporting on the Civil War in Libya, and sent some of the first dispatches about the Syrian Civil War from Turkey as a freelance journalist for Global Post. From 1999 to 2002, James Foley and I attended the Poets and Writers Program at UMASS-Amherst; ten years after our graduation, Jim lent me the money to buy server space to display the very first issues of Hinchas de Poesia on the Internet. He was not only courageous, morally, but he was prone to put his money where his mouth is. Librarians with Spines represents just another iteration of Jim's legacy, one that bends strongly towards works of social justice, and utilizes scholarship and education to combat inequality, disenfranchisement, and apathy.

Max Macias and I are primarily publishing this book to highlight the thoughtful, innovative work so many radical librarians are doing across the country. You know who you are. We see the work you concoct, day in-day out, at your information laboratories. However, we are also publishing this book so the U.S. publishing industry can get a clue, "buy a vowel," and commence to address the seminal role librarians of all colors play in educating and sustaining our entire demos, not just the communities that garner sizeable property-tax revenue. Furthermore, it would certainly prove fortuitous if we were actually able to nag the U.S. publishing industry into publishing more authors of color, or at least seek to reverse the entrenched, de facto Whiteness of the industry as a whole. It doesn't seem likely, but it is certainly true that the lack of people of color in the U.S. publishing industry inhibits the industry from publishing books that people of color write, read, and distribute.

It is mostly because of this glaring irregularity that we chose to bypass the current publishing model, and apply a do-it-yourself élan. Make no mistake about it, though, we are publishing this book because Max Macias ran a successful GoFundMe online campaign and raised $1,400 for funds directly relating to the publishing of this book. Furthermore, we are publishing this book because Autumn offered to design this book on her own dime, and provide the book its look, its aesthetic signature. In other words, during these difficult times, your capacity to say "yes" to challenges and opportunities the universe hurls your way can positively impact the trajectory of your resistance. Max and I started out as FaceBook friends, drawn together by adjacent career orbits, before we realized we both grew up skateboarding and listening to Hip Hop. I have never met Autumn, and yet something in her verve assured me she would prove an integral conspirator alongside Max.

Last, Max and I are publishing this book as a reminder to ourselves (and hopefully to you) about whom we Librarian for. Do we Librarian for corporate interests, or the common good? Do we Librarian for Title I barrios, or entitled vertical tracts? Do we Librarian for an immaculate vault, or a noisy garden? Do we Librarian for a drive-thru university, or one that services first-generation college students? Do we Librarian for Immigrants, or Nativists? Do we Librarian for an echo chamber of friends and peers on the Internet, or do we Librarian on behalf of people we might find vile and incorrigible? A librarian with a spine is a resourceful, buoyant information professional that feels an obligation to the community they serve, and, so, they act with that community's best interests in mind when they create programs, events, and initiatives.

Figure 3

# Introduction
## Max Macias

Libraries struggle with change. One reason libraries struggle with change is because they have not taken advantage of powerful changes that have occurred in libraries the past 30 years. These changes have not only taken place in libraries, but in US culture as well. The changes I'm talking about have to do with the fact that European-Americans will soon be a minority and are a minority already in certain places. These changes are economic, social, sexual, intellectual, and run across our society. This work hopes to capture some of these shifts, while also providing a snapshot of work being done by librarians all over our nation at this moment. The collection couldn't come at a more crucial time. With the rise of fascism in the US, it hopes to be a model for future endeavors by others and ourselves.

This work began as an idea, a phrase that popped into my head when ruminating on free Speech for librarians. Librarians have always been the defenders of intellectual freedom and free speech. It is ironic then, that librarians feel they can't speak out because it might hurt their careers, or their local library board might not agree with what they say, etc... I thought of all the librarians who had told me to keep my mouth shut, to not speak up, "...until you get situated in the right job."  While this is great advice for career advancement, oftentimes when librarians do get "there," they are bound by the aforementioned gags of career development now-- career maintenance.

Their hands are tied and their mouths sewn shut with money and 'power.'

US libraries have a real problem with diversity, equity and inclusion. This is because mainly middle class White people run libraries, Library Information Science (LIS). There are some ethnic minorities, but they tend to be those who can best survive in a world dominated by Whiteness. This trains them to adhere to the system of Whiteness that currently dominates US LIS. Those who assume roles that reinforce Whiteness in libraries are allowed to succeed, while those who rebel against Whiteness and other aspects of the so-called dominant culture, are ostracized.

The issue is, that Libraries need those who have been and are currently ostracized. We need these ideas, their energy, their creativity and their labor in order to progress. I want a library to represent all aspects of our culture--not just European American aspects. We need new ideas, new forms of representation, new forms of organization, new ways of thinking about information, and these new avenues will not spring forth from old waterways. This book is an attempt to be a catalyst for this needed change. We hope you enjoy it, find strength, inspiration, and will go out and create change after reading it.

Max Macias

Oregon

2/2017

Figure 4

Librarians With Spines

# Experiencing Whiteness of LIS Education: An Autoethnographic Account

Anthony Bishop
Borough of Manhattan
Community College

Kael Moffat
St. Martin's University

## Abstract

The assertion that librarianship, like American society in general, is steeped in whiteness is obvious to so many and discomforting to many more. While many in the library world have written about patterns of whiteness and mechanisms for producing and reproducing it in librarianship, the authors of this chapter have addressed the *experience* of whiteness in Library and Information Science education using autoethnographic methods. Both are recent graduates in the field and support efforts to make the field more inclusive. The interactive interview explores themes of classmates and classroom experience, LIS programs, culture, and identity.

## Experiencing Whiteness in LIS Education: An Autoethnographic Account

This paper started, as many do, at a restaurant with beer after the long first day of a conference, the 2015 Personal Librarian & First-Year Experience Librarian Conference at Case Western Reserve University. Three of us, the authors and a female colleague, went to dinner at the Happy Dog on Euclid Avenue. After ordering our gourmet hot dogs (Moffat had the veggie dog) and tater tots we sat at our table, listening to music, talking about Prince's recent death, the Black Lives Matter movement, and recent police shootings. As good academic librarians, we non-violently expressed dismay and even outrage over the shootings of so many men of color. We were particularly bothered by the choking death of Eric Garner by NYPD officers for selling cigarettes. Cigarettes, for Heaven's sake!

"Hey Tony," Moffat asked, "how does all this affect you as an educated African-American man?"

"You know, as a college-educated...grad-school educated professional, it might seem I would have less to fear than other black men," he noted, "but the fact is I still get kind of nervous around cops. Not petrified, but more nervous than I ought to be, especially when I haven't done anything wrong." After talking about Bishop's experience of "blackness" in every-day life, Moffat said that this generalized apprehension even haunted him in library school, and his first professional position. "I mean we're supposed to be all open and accepting in libraries, right? Isn't that all part of ALA ethics? Diversity, I mean." The rest of the evening's conversation centered on the various forms of intersectionalities we experienced in the profession: Bishop as an urban, African-American, early-career, male librarian; Moffat as a suburban, Caucasian, middle-aged, early-career, male librarian; Elizabeth as a rural, Caucasian, mid-career, female librarian.

The next evening, Bishop and Moffat went to Progressive Field to watch the Cleveland Indians play the Minnesota Twins. Walking to the ball park, we talked about how the city's vibe was far more hopeful, more positive than we had been lead to believe by the evening news and Rust Belt gloomers and doomers. Again, the evening involved dinner and beer in our upper-deck, first-base line seats that gave us a beautiful view of the downtown skyline.

(Bishop on the left and Moffat on the right at Progressive Field in Cleveland, May 13, 2016, photograph courtesy of Kael Moffat)

Naturally, being critical-theory minded, we fell to talking about the controversy around the ball club's mascot. "I'm glad they at least changed the logo on their hats to a C from that old cartoon of an Indian. Chief Wahoo, I think they call him," Moffat commented.

"Yeah, but it's still colonial discourse. The colonizers appropriating symbols from the colonized to assert power," Bishop responded.

"And to make the owners and players a *lot* of money," Moffat added. Homi Bhabha and Edward Said had definitely entered the conversation. Somewhere around the fourth inning, we came back to the previous night's conversation about race and librarianship.

"So how important is it to African-American students to see people with darker skin behind the desk?" Moffat asked.

"Oh man...that would be really important to a lot of black students. Even seeing a Latino behind the desk would be better because at least there's someone who could understand what it's like not being white," Bishop asserted (see Kim & Sin, 2008).

"So, were you the only student of color in your library classes?"

## Whiteness in Theory and in LIS Education

Throughout American history there has been a not-so-subtle advantage that comes with being white in America. The cultural infrastructure in America has favored Whiteness as a form of social promotion that allows Caucasians to benefit socially from their ethnicity, thus leading to the "Whiteness theory". Green, Sonn, and Matsebula (2007) took Frankenburg's definition of Whiteness as "'the production and reproduction of dominance rather than subordination, normativity rather than marginality, and privilege rather than disadvantage'" (as cited in Green, Sonn, & Matsebula, 2007, p. 390) and expounded on it. This definition is a useful starting point, yet "the meaning of Whiteness is also more complex than this" because Whiteness also "[renders] these positions and privileges invisible to White people" (Green, Sonn and Matsebula. 2007, p. 390).

The theory of Whiteness is not as simple as just exploring White privilege. Leonardo (2002) examined both the theory of Whiteness and White people. He wrote about the "difference between 'Whiteness' and 'White people': 'Whiteness' is a racial discourse, whereas the category 'White people' represents a socially constructed identity, usually based on skin color" (p. 31). The theory of "Whiteness" focuses more on the discourse of being White and the privilege that accompanies it. As Leonardo (2002) stated, "Whiteness is not a culture but a social concept" (p.32).

In applying this definition of "Whiteness" as a social concept, Leonardo (2002) provides the following characteristics of Whiteness:

>•*An unwillingness to name the contours of racism*': inequity (in employment, education, wealth, etc) is explained by reference to any number of alternative factors rather than being attributable to the actions of Whites.

•'The avoidance of identifying with a racial experience or group': Whiteness draws much of its power from 'Othering' the very idea of ethnicity. A central characteristic of Whiteness is a process of 'naturalization' such that White becomes the norm from which other 'races' stand apart and in relation to which they are defined. When White-identified groups *do* make a claim for a White ethnic identity alongside other officially recognized ethnic groups (e.g., as has been tried by the Ku Klux Klan in the US and the British National Party in England) it is the very exceptionality of such claims that points to the commonsense naturalization of Whiteness at the heart of contemporary political discourse.

•*The minimization of racist legacy*': seeking to 'draw a line' under past atrocities as if that would negate their continued importance as historic, economic and cultural factors. (p. 32)

The state of being White and the entity of Whiteness are vastly different. Whiteness provides a power dynamic that emanates from the entity it is displayed in. With this in mind examining whiteness requires a critical lens to gain a full understanding of how it works. Giroux (1997) observed that "the critical project that largely informs the new scholarship on 'Whiteness' rests on a singular assumption. Its primary aim is to unveil the rhetorical, political, cultural, and social mechanisms through which 'Whiteness' is both invented and used to mask its power and privilege" (p. 102).

The Calgary Anti-Racism Education Collective asserted that important aspects of Whiteness include social and political construction rooted in "ideology based in beliefs, values, behaviors, habits and attitudes, which result in the unequal distribution of power and privilege" (Understanding Whiteness, 2015), a state that exists in the library world as well as American culture at large. That Whiteness exists in librarianship and LIS education is an uncomfortable realization for some and an all-too-familiar barrier for others, reflected in the fact that, according to the ALA *Diversity Matters* report on race librarianship, white librarians make up approximately 87.9% of credentialed librarians despite Caucasians making up 74.3% of the population in general, meaning that librarians of color make up just 12.1% of credentialed librarians despite people of color making up 36.8% of the population at large  (ALA, 2012; US Census Bureau, 2010).

Gonzalez-Smith, Swanson & Tanaka (2014) observed that in academic librarianship, the number of academic librarians of color dropped to 0.5% to 13.9% between 2000 and 2010 even though the number of students of color enrolling in colleges and universities grew by 56% in that same period (p. 150). Thus, while US institutes of higher education and the United States itself are becoming *more* diverse, the American library world is becoming *less* so.

To address these striking gaps, the ALA and LIS programs in general have created various programs and initiatives to address corresponding deficits in the numbers of LIS graduate students of color, which Kim and Sin (2008) report as 11.3% of the LIS student population in general (p. 154). These programs have included the Spectrum Initiative (in which Bishop participated) and the Initiative to Recruit a Diverse Workforce, program-level scholarships, internships, recruitment programs and projects, as well as curriculum reforms (Kim & Sin, 2008; Hathcock 2015). In addition, a growing number of, "academic libraries also offer residency, internship, and fellowship programs for recruiting under represented groups in the LIS field" (Kim & Sin, 2008, p. 156). Galvan (2015) noted that barriers to librarianship for people of color include cultural barriers, lack of conspicuous leisure time for professional development, and lack of financial resources.

Candidates of color must be adept at performing Whiteness in interviews (including "professional" appearance and behavior), have had the opportunity to work non-paying or low-paying internships or some other form of library experience, as well as "access to wealth or tolerance for debt for tuition, professional membership, and service opportunities." Hathcock (2015) argued that these barriers even exist for programs designed to lessen these barriers for students of color, in her case the ARL's Career Enhancement Program.

## Autoethnography

In considering how to approach this chapter, we decided to take an autoethnographic approach, a method that calls attention not just to the presence of social phenomena but to the experience of them as well. Autoethnography combines two strains of writing that some might consider at odds with one another: autobiography and ethnography. Witkin (2014) characterized the method as "[residing] in the interstices between research and literature" (p. 3). Ellis and Bochner (2003) noted that this mode is often employed by writers who "zoom backward and forward, inward and outward," who find "distinctions between the personal and the cultural [becoming] blurred, sometimes beyond distinct recognition"; thus, it "is [a] genre of writing and research that displays multiple layers of consciousness, [explicitly] connecting the personal to the cultural" (p. 209).

As a philosophical stance, autoethnography can be a "powerful method for working with topics of diversity and identity" that can "invite readers into the lived experience of the presumed 'Other' and to experience it viscerally" (Boylorn and Orbe, 2014, p. 15). Autoethnographers use a wide variety of modes and formats not normally associated with academic writing. Ellis, Adams, and Bochner (2011) offered this partial list of possible formats: 1. indigenous/native ethnographies, 2. narrative ethnographies, 3. reflexive, dyadic interviews, 4. reflexive ethnographies, 5. layered accounts, 6. interactive interviews, 7. community authoethnographies, 8. co-constructed narratives, 9. personal narratives. Other formats include novels and dramas (Cann, C.N. & DeMeulenaere, E.J., 2012).

Autoethnographers could be criticized by their more empirically-minded colleagues as being self-absorbed, too emotional, too involved with the subject matter, and even narcissistic (Cann & DeMeulenaere, 2012; Ellis & Bochner, 2003). While autoethnographers are aware of such concerns and critiques, they recognize that there are compelling reasons to use the method despite such criticisms. On a most basic level, while we are all parts of social systems, we are all still individuals and experience those systems in individual ways--"Our lives are particular, but they also are typical and generalizable [to some degree], since we all participate in a limited number of cultures and institutions" (Ellis and Bochner, 2003, p.

229). Social and cultural phenomena are both individually and collectively experienced so autoethnographies highlight "epiphanies that stem from, or are made possible by, being part of a culture and/or by possessing a particular cultural identity" (Ellis, Adams, & Bochner, 2011), or set of cultural entities as it were.

By working at the intersection of autobiography and ethnography, autobiographers seek to "disrupt the binary of art and science" (Ellis, Adams, & Bochner, 2011) in order to illuminate aspects of shared experiences of the process(es) of identity (Bylorn & Orbe, 2014). The practice has close ties to emancipatory philosophical perspectives such as feminism (Wall, 2006), Marxism, and postcolonial theory, etc (Wall, 2006; Cann & DeMeulenaere, 2012). Ellis and Bochner (2003) asserted that autoethnography is a method that allows us to call attention to stories that may not be told or that may be co-opted by outsiders in order to "reduce [participants'] marginality" and invite readers to become "co-performers" and "encourage compassion and promote dialogue" (p. 223-225). Traditional analysis is secondary to the experience of social/cultural phenomenon. Our chapter is an interactive interview, which Ellis, Adams, and Bochner (2011) pointed out can be used to used to specifically address sensitive and provocative questions and are "situated within the context of emerging and well-established relationships."

## Interactive interview on Whiteness in LIS education

Cann and DeMeulenaere (2012) argued that "critical co-constructed" autoethnographic texts such as this chapter enact Paulo Freire's notion of praxis, or knowledge and understanding that is gained through actual experience and practice. This format allows each participant to offer their own "testimonial" (as Bishop called it) in the same space/ document, yielding co-constructed knowledge with the belief that such a combined narrative will "encourage us [both Bishop and Moffat, as well as readers] to better understand and learn from each other while showing the interconnectedness of human experience" (Boylorn & Orbe, 2014, p.15).

We believe that this format can help us shed richer light on the experience of Whiteness in LIS education through the "stories" of one who has benefited from Whiteness (and believes in a much more inclusive social vision) and of one who has had to struggle against it. The interview was conducted via shared Google Drive documents, to allow each other to time to reflect on the questions, to ask follow up questions, and revisit and flesh out our answers. We also talked via telephone, email, and instant messaging. Through the interview, three broad themes emerged: 1) classmates and courses, 2) LIS programs, 3) culture and identity.

## Classmates and Courses

*Moffat* What was one of the first experiences that affirmed to you that the library world reflects the Whiteness of general American society? Overtly or covertly.

> *Bishop* My first experience of racism I dealt with in LIS took place during my first full semester in my program. A classmate (White) refused to be on a team with me and I knew it was for no other reason than my ethnicity because during the on-campus session, the classmate avoided any interaction with me and I overheard ethnically derogatory statements by him.

*Moffat* What were the statements, if you can remember them? I'm interested here because I think recalling the language itself is significant... and evocative.

> *Bishop* The specific statements the classmate said to me was, "I am not comfortable working with you." I asked why and he could not explain he said. I already knew why. He then went to the instructor and asked to be moved.

*Moffat* Were there specific artifacts or assignments that you felt highlighted your non-Whiteness?

> *Bishop* I can say that a majority of the work we had in the program in classes such as Reference and Community Informatics dealt a lot with issues of patron diversity. I also took a course on diversity in LIS that of course focused on issues of "non-Whiteness". The

class was an elective. That was the great thing about my program. Only two classes are required and the rest of the 30 credit hours are elective. Other courses did not address diversity directly.

**Moffat** Were there any concepts you studied in classes that triggered an "Oh...this is Whiteness" response? (That may be worded poorly, but it's the best I can think of right now).

**Bishop** Not concepts per se, but just covering topics in general that served as a constant reminder of how "White" the library profession is.

**Moffat** Could you give an example here? Whiteness tends to be so hidden that these subtle points can be darn near impossible to see.

**Bishop** Have you never encountered classmates exhibiting racist viewpoints in your LIS program? If so, did you confront them or stay silent?

**Moffat** The school I went to also relied on hybrid classes and there were relatively few of us that lived in town. We got together for classes and every so often between weekends, so I got to know them reasonably well. We were all white, though one of them had a biracial child. My cohort on the whole was likewise pretty white. We had one student who was Latina. I asked the program coordinator about that and he said they simply didn't get that many applications from students of color.

I would say the most exclusive comments I heard from classmates were complaints about having a hard time understanding two of our professors who were from India and still had thick accents. The first time this happened, I said, "Come on guys, we can do better than that." One of the women gave me a subtle oh-I-got-caught look and said, "You're right." I thought my fellow students understood that my comment was directing attention to the idea that complaining about someone's accent is a subtle form of racism, but as I think about that incident now, I see that it could have been interpreted as just me just trying to be polite and courteous. It could have not been interpreted as a caution against racism. I wonder now if my decision came out of my assumption that they would know that I was trying to make a specific point about race...but, I think it also came out of being such a new group that I didn't want to step on any toes. In retrospect,

I think I ought to have been more open about why I objected.

It did happen a second time and when I called it out, one of my classmates turned to me with a bit of exasperation and said something to the effect of "We're just having a bit of fun." This time I pointed out that complaining about someone's accent can be racist. "I'm not saying you're racist, just that this behavior is," I said. I admitted that I found the teacher hard to understand, especially when he was speaking enthusiastically, but I pointed out that his PowerPoint slides were quite clear and he had a circular speaking style so he stated his point several times. One of the other students mentioned noticing a similar speaking style when teaching English in Korea. I got the rolled eyes reaction and we refocused on the assignment. I think I made my point, though. I don't remember any complaints afterwards, but I will say a couple students were a bit stand-offish, so I must have struck a nerve. It took me a little while to be able to articulate that what bothered me about these two incidents was an aspect of Whiteness: the expectation that you can complain about or make fun of something like someone's accent and not have it read as offensive.

> **Bishop**   During your time in your LIS program have you experienced any situation where either yourself, other students or teachers and/ or administration promoted some issue or program centered around diversity?

*Moffat*   That's an interesting question and the answer is yes and no. In my first year, I worked as a library intern at a local high school and helped to create displays for Native American Heritage Month, Black History Month, and Women's History Month. I managed to put a couple of images of Leonard Peltier in the Native American display, though my supervisor nixed putting up a picture that included the words, "Free Leonard Peltier." She did acknowledge sympathy, but didn't want to upset the administration. I probably could have, and maybe should have pressed the issue further, but I was a grad student with children, so making too big a deal of things seemed like a bad idea. For the Black History Month display, I tried to keep the focus on Civil Rights leaders--their images, books, etc. I'd just re-read some of James Baldwin's essays, so I put Notes of a Native Son front and center. For the second year, I was a Graduate Assitant (GA) at the college library and we had a number of diversity displays and programming. One of the big events at the library for several years running was an Arabic Students' Associations event in the library. I believe the event coincided with the hajj, part of the pilgrimage to Mecca.

But as far as the library school itself, I don't recall anything. I had a professor who was of Chinese descent who posted something on his door about Chinese New Year, but nothing official as I recall. Diversity was something we brought up in class, but it didn't seem to be a central concern.

## LIS Programs

*Moffat* What has been the role of mentors in your LIS experience? Who are/were your mentors? Did you select them?

> *Bishop* Being a Spectrum scholar (ALA diversity scholarship program), mentors were provided to me from the beginning of my graduate program. I personally never took on a mentor, though, because I never felt a connection with the person I was initially set up with. And, as a result, I have mostly travelled in this program and profession on my own. My mentors come from my other academic degrees. I have personally found it very difficult to connect, on a deep-level, with other people of color in this profession, in terms of mentor/ee relationships, so I navigate the waters autonomously.

*Moffat* Can you expand on this? For me, this is a key issue, especially in light of April Hathcock's (2015) piece, in which she talks about the mixed blessing of the Spectrum Scholar program.

> *Bishop* When I was initially placed with a mentor it was a very dry email interaction that initiated the relationship. I knew from the tone and social and cultural background of the mentor that there would be no true connection from an experiential point of view. I have met other black male librarians at conferences, but none have been from an urban environment like the southside of Chicago. I find my three demographic outliers: black, urban, and heterosexual to be a very difficult fit in terms of finding mentors. I am not saying other people who fall under those demographic categories do not exist in the LIS profession, but we are few and far between and that

makes finding true mentors very difficult.

*Moffat* You've mentioned concerns over ALA's diversity issues, how did you "discover" those concerns in your program?

> *Bishop* Being a Spectrum scholar placed me in the loop of ALA matters and I found out very early in my experience about its diversity initiatives which addresses the issues of diversity as a whole in the profession. I have been privileged to serve on two diversity committees in ALA and I see clearly now what the issues are.

*Moffat* One or two specific points you want to make on this? I think this another place where your perspective could be really helpful to white readers for whom libraryland is a "natural" space.

> *Bishop* One of the biggest issues I have encountered around diversity is at conferences (I have attended six in the past year) that address these issues. I find that the same types of librarians attend these conferences: lower-level librarians with little or no authority to affect change and in turn the conferences become large venting sessions where great ideas are discussed but no real action can come out of it. That is why I proposed the committee on diversity and inclusion and the workshop on diversity training at my current job. I wanted to get people in position of authority involved in the discussion so true change could come.

> *Bishop* What does diversity and inclusion mean to you in LIS programs?

*Moffat* I think diversity means I go into a classroom and find men and women of different ethnicities, sexual orientation, etc. Some of those, are admittedly hard to "see," but they need to be there. I think it would also include more than passing reference to serving diverse populations, but would make that a learning objective in each course. Try to address it many times in different courses. That may be harder to do in some courses, but it could be a goal. Doing so might counter the "token diversity element" that I think we see sometimes. Of course, for me, being familiar with critical theory going into my program gave me a perspective that other students may not have had--I had earned an MA in English before doing my MLS degree. I'm sure that affected how I think about my experience as a white LIS student.

> **Bishop** Do you believe LIS programs, as a whole, promote diversity in the curriculum? In what way?

**Moffat** The concept of diversity certainly gets airtime, so to speak. We addressed it in my class on reference services and there was a chapter on serving diverse patrons in the book, so there was that level of attention, but I would have liked more. There was a class on serving diverse populations, but I don't remember seeing it offered, although it may have been and I couldn't fit it into my schedule. I believe the history of libraries class looked at different cultural approaches to information organization, but I didn't take that class. I read about the topic. I do remember a conversation with a fellow student in which we talked about how most of what we were learning seemed very Anglo-Americancentric. That was the student I talked about earlier who had taught in Korea. Come to think of it, in my library management class, we did have a chapter on "Managing Diversity," which I thought was fairly positive, asserting that "Corporations that build strong, diverse organizations reap numerous dividends" (Daft, 2010, p. 348). But it didn't really come up in other courses.

The question of exclusion also stood out to me when I was the blog editor for our Student Chapter of the American Library Association (SCALA) chapter and I received a submission from a professor who had written a narrative about traveling back in time to 18th century China and having a tour of the library and tea with a librarian. The narrative, of course, was a vehicle for discussing that particular form of information organization, noting that Western conceptions of organization are just some of many possible organizations and that the very concept of organization is culturally bound.

> **Bishop** How do you view "Whiteness" in LIS graduate programs in terms of ideology, promotion and presence?

**Moffat** I received a lot of encouragement from my professors, including professors of color, and I really appreciated that--I was in my 40s when I went to library school, so any encouragement was appreciated--but there were times when I wondered how many students of color get that level and quality of encouragement. I really hope there would be the same level, but

I can't say. I didn't get to see it.

An aspect of Whiteness in my program that concerned me was professor turnover in the department. While I was in the program, four professors had their contracts terminated: three were Asian or of Asian descent, and the other was a woman. A fifth was a Japanese American man who was there as a VAP but was offered an administrative position rather than a full-time teaching position. I thought the program had really good gender balance, but not ethnic balance. I would not be comfortable saying the department was overtly racist, but there certainly seemed to be strong evidence of institutional or structural racism...the kind that's hard to spot. And that bothered me. I've mentioned before, that my cohort was really quite white, but the one after mine was a bit more diverse with at least one African-American young woman and a middle-aged Indian woman I already knew--we'd been colleagues at the high school where I used to teach. Of course, I can only speak from a limited perspective, but I would have to say I did see a good deal of subtle Whiteness in library school.

I have to admit to contributing to this culture, though. When I was a GA, I helped hire another GA to replace a colleague who had graduated. The two finalists were young women, a Native American student and a bubbly White student. Both students had outstanding resumes and had already been admitted to the program. The Native American student had been to campus once before (though I didn't meet her at that point), but had to interview with us via Skype. The interview was supposed to be in person, but circumstances changed. She seemed rather stiff and tentative. The other committee members had met her previously and commented on how different she had seemed in person. The other candidate actually interviewed in person when she visited campus. She interviewed very well. We ended up hiring the second student and she ended up doing a really good job, but I've wondered since then whether our reaction to the first candidate wasn't shaded by our Whiteness. She had made a strong first impression, but not a strong second impression. I can completely understand her nervousness and wonder if that was part of her affect in the interview. I wonder sometimes if I should have made more of a case for her in the interest of inclusion. There are many White women in the library world, but relatively few Native Americans (Bourg, 2014). I wonder if I had met her in person before if that might have changed my mind. I'd like to think it would have.

> **Bishop** Do you feel that you have benefited in the LIS program in terms of admittance or any other way due to your whiteness?

**Moffat** To be sure, I have benefited from my status as a healthy, White, heterosexual male with a more or less middle-class background. I know this has helped. Before moving to Washington, I delivered a paper in Oregon and got to know a really...beautiful person is the best thing that comes to mind, a Pacific Islander, a community college librarian. We seemed to get along from right off the bat so I think he felt comfortable saying to me, "I can see that you are excited to get to your job, but I want to tell you something that will help you appreciate your opportunity. In the Pacific Northwest, there are literally hundreds of unemployed and underemployed librarians. It was your teaching experience that really set you apart." I appreciated his comment and encouragement, but at the same time it came to mind that some of those unemployed and underemployed are probably people of color and women, even women of color--I've had that confirmed. I would like to think that my hard work and teaching experience and skill play into the fact that I got hired, but I have to concede that my white skin played a role, as well. And that is a bit discomforting.

## Culture and identity

**Moffat** Have you had to "justify" your decision to become a librarian to people in your family or your non-White friends?

> **Bishop** Absolutely! My friends and family didn't understand why I wanted to pursue an LIS career . The perception of the profession is totally white and as a person of color from an urban setting, the thought of librarianship is totally foreign to my demographic. I find myself justifying all the time my rationale behind pursuing the LIS degree initially. But, I personally see my role in this profession as a learning tool for all.

**Moffat** Can you give an illustrative example? I think this would really make a strong point, especially for White readers.

**Bishop**  My close friends laughed at me when I told them I was pursuing a graduate degree in LIS. Their common theme was, "Why do you want to stack books with old White people for a living?" I was mocked for about a year as I entered the program. This created a difficult dynamic between cultural and self-doubt because of the racism I was experiencing from my cohort and the mocking I received from my friends.

**Moffat**  Do you see any cultural barriers to becoming a librarian that may not be immediately apparent to outsiders? So...I guess my question here is getting at whether you have experienced pressures from non-Whites.

**Bishop**  I can say you certainly feel like an outsider in this profession as an African-American, hetorsexual male from an urban environment. The cultural barriers are more built in I would say. My upbringing and experience is unique from others in this profession and it has crafted my personality in a way that stands out from others. I am very opinionated on issues of race and inclusion openly and that openness is not shared by most people I encounter in the profession. I find that people in the profession love to discuss diversity in "safe spaces" of social media groups, but many don't have the courage to look in the eye of authority and address the issue directly. At Syracuse, I did just that in a meeting with the Dean where I proposed the creation of a diversity and inclusion committee and diversity training workshop which ultimately got approved and funded. I have been at LIS conferences where the issues were raised about racial issues but people would close those issues by stating "but I can't say anything because of fear of losing my job." I have no fear whatsoever of reprisal in this profession and I speak my mind accordingly, but I find I am the only one with this courage.

**Bishop**  How do you view your own "whiteness" in the LIS profession in terms of advantages fair and/or unfair you may have had or are currently experiencing?

**Moffat**  As I've said before, I'm convinced it played some degree in my being hired. I don't know anything about the other candidates. For me the interview process was generally "friendly territory" because my hiring committee was predominantly White with only one person of color, a professor outside the library. So, for me, the interview seemed to flow quite well and comfortably since I saw faces that looked more or less like mine. To turn a question posed by Berry (2004), I was "in the professional company of people of my race." I more or less understood the hidden codes of conversation, conditions of familiarity, and expected language and behaviors. I've imagined that if the hiring committee were of a different ethnic make up, I might have felt more apprehensive. Although, now that I say that, I recognize that I might still be in a privileged position since I fit many of the expected "norms" of dominant culture.

> **Bishop**  Do you consider yourself a proponent of diversity? In what ways?

**Moffat**  I would like to think of myself as a proponent of diversity. I vote for candidates who openly advocate for diversity, especially when the options include people of color. I try to teach my kids about diversity and inclusion and I hope I've been successful in that. I try to cultivate diversity in my friendships, as well.

On the level of librarianship, I have tried to use my role as a marketing librarian to call attention to diverse populations on campus. We recently invited the Latino Student Association to put up a very colorful dia de los muertos shrine in the library. Also, at the beginning of this semester, I posted a whiteboard question, inviting users to write "Welcome to the library" in their own language and loved the response we got! We got responses in Arabic, Chinese, Korean, Portugese, Spanish, French, German, and Russian.

I also try to be a voice for diversity around campus. I am the social science and women's studies librarian and am trying to help with the WS program's efforts to give itself a bigger voice on campus. I also recently participated in a panel on Native American issues, giving the voice of a white ally. These are small gestures in the grand scheme of things, but I am trying to pay attention to other voices and help give them airtime (again, that broadcast metaphor).

> **Bishop**  With the percentages of persons of color so low in LIS graduate programs and the profession as a whole, what do you think LIS programs can do to change these percentages?

***Moffat*** I have thought a good deal about this. My adoptive mentor in library school was a man of Japanese descent who experiences a very different set of interstices than me. Working with him was a wonderful experience because we talked a number of times about diversity in librarianship--different forms of it. Racial, health, sexual orientation, etc. He felt that more concerted efforts need to be made in recruiting and I certainly agree, but something that I see is crucial is a cultural shift that I think needs to be made.

I wonder if there are African-American and other non-white undergraduate students who can't see themselves as "cultural workers," to use Henry Giroux's (1992) term. Librarianship is certainly a line of cultural work, but a sticky one especially as we think of its educative function, since schools are "political sites" (Giroux, 1992, p. 152) and part of what Louis Althusser (1970) called the "educational Ideological State Apparatus"--this connection is forcefully argued in Bales and Engle (2012). But libraries, like schools, can also be sites of liberation. The lesson I took from my students, though, is that there needs to be cultural shift that allows more non-White students to see themselves in cultural work. Of course, dominant culture wants to affirm that that is already happening--the ALA has certainly used the language of inclusion--but people of color in librarianship are the exception to the rule, with some having miniscule representation, as Bourg points out (2014).

To be honest, I don't know that I have any grand answer here. Cultural shifts are huge and can't be manufactured, only encouraged. LIS programs can't create this shift from scratch, but they can contribute to it by openly inviting students of color, by presenting more images of minority librarians. They do that now, of course, but it seems that many of these images seem to feature librarians as "professionals" in nice suits and nice prim settings. They often also seem to be separated from others. I'm thinking of images of Trevor Dawes (former ACRL president). Sure, he dresses "professionally," but he still has his dreadlocks and unorthodox facial hair. Yet, pictures I've seen of him are just him alone. I wonder how it would strike an African-American young man or Latina (thinking back on my students) to see images of librarians who look more like them interacting authentically with other librarians and with students. Both non-White and

White. I would think that that could be quite powerful. I also wonder about how much recruitment is targeted at urban state schools, historical black colleges, tribal colleges, etc. where the opportunity to engage with students of color are higher. It was heartening to find as I've been researching for this chapter that Kim and Sin's (2008) work with library students of color and recent graduates also make similar recommendations. In the end, we have to figure out ways to make the library world one in which people of color can really see themselves.

# Engaging the Future of Zine Librarianship

Ann Matsushima Chiu

## Abstract

As zine culture is popularized, the need for alternative publications in public and academic libraries is no longer something to be argued for, but rather something to be expected. The role of the zine librarian shifts from forming and establishing zine libraries to a longevity struggle of creating sustainable zine library models. The significance of the study lies within the specialized knowledge, current practices, and lived experiences, with an emphasis on the need for institutional buy-in, succession planning, and continually building community within zine librarians networks.

Drawing from a series of interviews, in addition to zine library literature, this research seeks to engage with the future of "zinebrarianship," endearingly dubbed by zine librarians. Librarian Cathy Camper of Multnomah County Public Library (Portland, Oregon) and Librarian Jenna Freedman of Barnard Library (New York City, New York) add their voices to the scholarship of zine libraries through their experience as zine librarians. They are still hard at work seeking to create sustainable, accessible, and effective legacies for zines, zine libraries, and the ways in which patrons use and navigate zines.

## Engaging the Future of Zine Librarianship

*"I'm arguing for a relationship between people and places--the places we populate and the places within we circulate--in order to suggest that we not only define these spaces but are also, in part, defined by them."*

- Adela C. Licona, Zines in Third Space

## Introduction

Through a small sample of participants, the following qualitative study seeks to unpack the interviews of two zine librarians, one of whom works within a county public library system, and the other in an academic research library. This study reveals Librarians Cathy Camper and Jenna Freedman tackling difficult questions about budget cuts and layoffs. They both seek to inspire sustainable legacies for zine library collections beyond the libraries that they work for. While working as a librarian in an academic research library may differ from that of working as a librarian in the county public library system, the concerns of zine librarians, despite the system and institution they work for, are surprisingly similar.

Drawing from a series of interviews, library literature, zine scholarship, and the author's personal involvement in current zine culture, this research seeks to engage the future of zine librarianship. Camper and Freedman express similar concerns and challenges for zine libraries and zine librarians, as revealed through their specialized knowledge, current practices, and years of experience as zinesters, as librarians, and as zine librarians. While this study is not a study on zines in the library, it has proven useful to understand zine history and context that both the author and the interviewees come from. All create zines, participate in zine culture, and are active members of the zine community, as well as are currently working in libraries, and actively engaged with zine librarianship.

This study engages the following questions: How can zine librarians argue for continued funding and institutional support? How do they balance their role as a zine librarian with their main jobs as librarians? What are the plans for succession, and how can we be certain that the zine library collections stay intact, relevant, and functioning so that these libraries of alternative, countercultural media can be preserved for generations to come?

## Zines: The What and the Why

From its first page, Zines! Vol. I sought to define the history of zines, and reveal the inner lives of self-publishing through feature interviews with zinesters of the 1980s and 1990s. Editor of the punk zine Search and Destroy and Zines! Vol. I & II, V. Vale of V/Search Publications describes the "DO IT YOURSELF" (DIY) ethos of self-published and cheaply xeroxed publications effective in its ability to be "a grassroots reaction to a crisis in the media landscape" (Vale, 1996, 4). Zines require active creators who, in publishing unconventional, alternative, and political to personal topics, challenge and circumnavigate the mainstream media while offering a strong critique to what is being written, produced, and consumed.

Zines! Vol. I is commonly referred to as, "the first book on the zine movement" with Vale explaining in an interview with Clamor Magazine,

> *I put out the first book and then about a dozen corporate books on zines came out after mine. Mine was the first to market* (Zass, 2001, 45).

One of the ways that sets Zines! Vol. I and II apart from the other books on zines that were published between 1997-1999 like Chip Rowe's Book of Zines: Readings from the Fringe (1997), Stephen Duncombe's seminal work Notes for Underground: Zines and the Politics of Alternative Culture (1997), or R. Seth Friedman's The Factsheet Five Zine Reader: The Best Writing from the Underground World of Zines (1997) was that Vale published in-depth and uncensored interviews with zinesters. Zines! carved out space to allow zinesters to speak their minds and passions.

Vale explains why he prefers the free-ranging interview format versus a well structured research thesis.

> *The freedom that an interview gives you is the freedom to range widely over topics all over the universe...I mean, it's harder to*

*attain that freedom in a strictly written piece, because you're supposed to stick to the point, you're supposed to have a thesis you're developing, a few supporting thesis, and then a conclusion at the end which allegedly wraps up the way you started...They all demand certain formulas for their writing, which I resent. I'd just love to read a piece that goes all over the map and doesn't necessarily have to reflect a structural unity in which the end recapitulates the beginning* (Zass, 2001, 45-46).

In this way, Vale maintains the uncensored zine punk aesthetic and remains true in V/Search's mission to document underground culture and unconventional creatives as they produce their artistic work.

Vale's 1996 "From the Editor" introduction reveals that the limitations of the subcultural production of zines are within issues of accessibility: in that zines can be more difficult to find and access. Vale notes that "some of the greatest zines ever produced are virtually impossible to obtain today" (Vale, 1996, 5). Vale's critique on the difficulty of unearthing zines is that zines are often created and maintained in underground and specialized community networks, and for the outside consumer, zines may be nearly invisible, thus impossible to find and purchase. Access to zines were improved through networks such as the zine review serial Factsheet Five (1982-1998), Mimi Thi Nguyen's zine Race Riot Project Directory (2004), Alex Wrekk's Stolen Sharpie Revolution (2003), Grrrl Zines a Go Go (2002), etc. Within these zine networks, zine enthusiasts are able to connect with zine makers or zine publication distribution networks called 'distros'.

Zine scholar Adela C. Licona (2012) places feminist and queer zinesters of color at the forefront of Zines in Third Space: Radical Cooperation and Borderlands Rhetoric. Licona's scholarship subverts the notion that zines are produced by mostly white, heterosexual, cis-gendered, middle-class individuals by centering queer creators of color that write and produce zines with the purpose of "advocat[ing] for change based on identified affinities and intersections of oppression, injustice, and inequity" (Licona, 2012, 2). The zines that Licona focuses on are:

> *...grassroots literacies meant to effect change through the circulation of information and the production of new practices, perspectives, and knowledges. They are sites where traditional knowledges circulate and something collide with newer knowledges to produce innovative and informed practices. They are action-oriented, feminist and sometimes queer-identified; they are conscious of race, radicalization, sex, sexualization, gender, and class* (Licona, 2012, 2).

In Licona's footnotes, Stephen Duncombe's research on the subject of zines is acknowledged, and places Zines in Third Space within a similar "political potential" of "provok[ing] the kind of awareness that changes practices in community contexts" (Licona, 2012, 143).

Zines acting as provocateurs, agitating and provoking for change, resistance, and revolution, remains a potent reason that zines are useful tools for revealing hidden discourses in our libraries. Zines are often elusive in their definition, as the zine maker's unpredictable nature and their resistance to rules of form and content, with the zine acting as a direct challenge against mainstream ideals and lifestyles. The zines of interest within the collections of Barnard Library and Multnomah County Public Library are zines that represent counter narratives to the larger subcultural movement of zine making. We borrow the works of Solorzano and Yosso (2002) for the concept of counter storytelling within zine culture as:

> *...a method of telling the stories of those people whose experiences are not often told (i.e., those on the margins of society). The counter-story is also a tool for exposing, analyzing, and challenging the majoritarian stories of racial privilege. Counter-stories can shatter complacency, challenge the dominant discourse on race, and further the struggle for racial reform* (Solorzano and Yosso, 2002, 32).

Librarians seek to locate and purchase alternative materials for their libraries, in order to expand their ephemera collections, and to increase the number of autobiographical counter narratives from underrepresented and underserved people: women, people of color, poor and working class people, people who identified as LGBTQIA, people with disabilities, punks, teens, the elderly and sick, etc.

Some zines, such as the Asian American pop culture publication Giant Robot or feminist publication Bitch, eventually became largely circulated glossy magazines, but these were special cases. Many zinesters reject the notion of a larger circulation and commercial focus, and find pride in the black-and-white photocopied handmade pamphlets, placing more value on a bartering and trade culture than a monetary commercial sale. Zines often times are conduits within punk and political scenes, and often times house hand drawn fliers advertising local shows or gatherings, which are distributed at info shops, venue spaces, and zine fests. Due to small print runs and circulation, typically ranging from five to 1,000 copies, zines are primarily self-distributed amongst friends and small networks (Freedman, 2006, 36).

In terms of physicality, zines are commonly photocopied and saddle stitched with the size and shape of zines depending on its maker. Because zines often occupy an ephemeral and personal nature, each zine represents a specific time, place and story. Yet it is the nature of flux that allows zines to represent particular moments, movements, and histories, by those who are experiencing it firsthand. It is in this sense, that Freedman compares zines to quilts and other forms of outsider art (Koppel, 2006, 1).

Authorship for zines range from being single authored, from a collaboration of a group or collective, or as a compilation of many authors centering on specific themes or narratives. Freedman notes

> *...that compared to 1960s-style alternative press publications, zines tend to be authored by individuals, not groups and are thus more personal* (Freedman, 2009, 53).

Zines are commonly produced by those in their twenties, though zinesters can be of any age. Zinesters in their adult years make zines on work, social justice, mental health, parenting, politics, geek culture, or have continued to create zines since their youth.

## Literature Review

Much of the literature about zine libraries focuses upon collection development, the acquisition of non-traditional print materials, reconciling challenges in cataloging zines, and zine library programming. Sandy Berman (1976), Jim Danky (1981), and Chris Dodge (1995) champion the early cause of zine librarianship, creating a convincing argument for the role and reason for alternative publications and zines in libraries.

From 1984 to 2002, Berman, a cataloging librarian in Minnesota, and Danky, a periodicals librarian for the State Historical Society of Wisconsin, co-published Alternative Library Literature, which in the 1998/1999 Biennial copy, features the art of Cathy Camper, who is one of the two zine librarians interviewed in this study. The cover art is a collaged image of woman who is having Dewey Decimal classifications tattooed upon her body. The tattooed dewey numbers represent the unconventional topics that Berman and Danky published articles about, like 305.90664: Lesbian and Gay Studies, 323.42: The 1961 Commission of Civil Rights or 320.57: Anarchists. Through Camper's Dewey Decimal art, the reader can decipher what topics and issues Berman and Sanford advocate for.

Amongst the various articles published in Alternative Library Literature in the 1998/1999 edition, "Your Friendly Neighborhood Infoshop" and "Street Newspapers Create Lively Alternative to Establishment Media" address alternative publications such as zines, political pamphlets and street newspapers. Zines were just one part of the bigger vision to collect alternative media in order to represent marginalized and underserved voices, or to represent the uniqueness of a particular region or library collection.

Julie Bartel furthers Dodge's argument by stating in the seminal From A to Zine: How to Build a Winning Zine Collection in Your Library that

> If collections do not offer a wide variety of viewpoints, topics, media, and styles, library nonusers just might be right in thinking they will not find what they're after at the library (Bartel, 2004, 35).

Bartel explains that one of the main reasons for collecting zines can be to better serve patrons who may feel alienated, ignored, or not view the library has a space that will cater or house their interests or perspectives. This view of better serving patrons is intrinsic to good librarianship, and when applied to library collections makes for a good case for adding alternative materials to the existing collection. Yet within From A to Zine, Bartel describes the process of obtaining a sizable collection of alternative materials as "simply unmanageable" and thus decided to:

> *...focus on zines as a format, rather than on the content of publications... [in order to] build a coherent and manageable (though I use that term loosely) collection and give legitimacy and publicity to zine publishers* (Bartel, 2004, 47).

While many of these articles are aimed towards both the barefoot (non- degreed) and degreed librarian interested in the potential of starting a zine collection within their own particular library system, there appears to be a gap in recent articles between 2006 to 2014 on the future for zine librarianship. Yet Tkach and Hank's (2014) quantitative study of zines and zine collections in Association of Research Libraries (ARL) and Canadian Association of Research Libraries (CARL) argues that, "It is time to sound the call to collect zines once again" (Tkach and Hank 2014, 18). The study found a lack of academic libraries with zines appearing on their online catalogs (only 23% of ARL, 14% of CARL). The study concluded that the difficult process for collecting and cataloging zines is, perhaps, what detours academic libraries from including zines in existing collections. Also to note, there is a lack of zine coverage in the LIS curriculum so aspiring professionals are not aware of zines unless they have personal knowledge and/or experience.

Interestingly, within the last several years, authors such as Woodbrook and Lazarro (2013), Lymn (2013) and Honma (2016) focused attention upon the archival perspective for zine collections. This shift from articles regarding zines in libraries to zines in archives further emphasizes how increasingly necessary it is to clarify the differences between the goals of a zine archive from that of a zine library. It is within this difference that many zine librarians might find themselves in the "great tension" between issues of preservation and access of zines (Woodbrook and Lazzaro, 2013, 8).

It is important to add that scholarship on zines created by people of color has grown since 2009, with a chapter on intersectional identities in "grrrl zines" in Alison Piepmeier's Girl Zines: Making Media, Doing Feminism (2009). Additionally, Adela Licona's Zines in Third Space: Radical Cooperation and Borderlands Rhetoric (2012) explores feminist of-color zines that "advocate for change based on identified affinities and intersections of oppression, injustice, and inequity" (Licona, 2012, 2). And most recently, Todd Honma's essay "From Archives to Action: Zines, Participatory Culture, and Community Engagement in Asian America" (2016) addresses using zines in the archives as a way to connect with living history and embedding community action into zine making (Honma, 2016, 37). While Piepmier, Licona, and Honma's work does not directly address zine librarianship, it does address the production of zines, the labor behind zines, and how zines can be used as subversive tools for community action and change. This in turn affects how zine librarianship develops programming and collection development around their zine collections.

Using the zine library literature as a guide to gauge interest from the library community in zine librarianship, it is worth noting that since 2005, there has been an increase of articles documenting zines in libraries. Freedman states as well,

> *I do notice that there is, not a newfound, but a renewed passion for zines in the last few years. I feel that Barnard Zine Library is just part of it; we are just part of the zeitgeist* (Freedman, 2014, Interview).

Alongside this renewed passion is a trend in how zines, zines in libraries, and zine librarians are covered and perceived. Perhaps this comes from the alternative, countercultural, and punk backgrounds of many of the zine librarians, but is important to emphasize that these collections are the result of years of hard work, dedication, and passion, and are not simply the newest fleeting trendy thing to do on the librarian scene.

While a number of articles cover zines in libraries over the course of years (Herrada 1994, Dodge 1995, Chepesiuk 1997, Zobel 1999, Kucsma

2002, Stoddart and Kiser 2004, Gisonny and Freedman 2006), it appears that zine librarianship scholarship is entering a time where the original founders of zine collections need to start thinking about future succession plans for zine library collections. This study seeks to activate and direct zine scholarship to think forward upon how current and veteran zine librarians are planning, mentoring, and passing down their specialized knowledge to the next generation of zine librarians. These interviews with zine librarians Cathy Camper and Jenna Freedman provided evidence that while academic libraries might treat their zine collections differently than public libraries, there are striking similarities in the issues and challenges within zine librarianship as a whole.

## Methodology

For this study on zine librarianship, the sample of two librarians were interviewed for two one-hour increments, along with personal correspondence, and interacting closely in the zine community. While the two participants are practicing degreed librarians, who are zine librarians in addition to their other professional duties, which include reference, instruction, communications, marketing, and outreach. The participants were chosen based upon their current librarian positions; one in the public library system, and the other in an academic library.

The first participant is Cathy Camper. Camper has been involved with zines in libraries since the late 1990s at the Minneapolis Public Library in Hennepin, Minnesota. There she began a small zine collection through donations of a local zine distro (Hubbard, 2005, 353). Camper currently works for the Multnomah County Public Library (MCPL) in Portland, Oregon. She joined the Zine Librarians group for MCPL in 2006 as the group was proposing selection policies, programming, cataloging, etc. in order to launch a countywide zine library initiative. Camper now used her position as a Youth Services: Outreach to Schools Librarian to teach and host zine workshops to mainly middle school aged youth. She is also an active member of the Portland-based Women of Color Zine Collective, who often writes of her experiences as a mixed race Arab American.

The second participant in this study is Jenna Freedman. Freedman has written numerous articles on zine librarianship, as well as being a willing interviewee in several articles in the last ten years. Her primary title at Barnard College in New York City is Associate Director of Communications, where she is a Research and Instruction Librarian as well. In 2003, she pitched the idea of a zine collection to colleagues and bosses, where she then gained the institutional support of Barnard Library to start the Barnard Zine Library. In addition to her work at Barnard, Freedman is a very active in the zine librarian community, moderating the Zine Librarians listserv, attending various zine librarian (un)conferences and chairs various planning committees for zine fests and zine events around town.

## Findings

While working as a librarian in an academic research library differs from that of working as a librarian in a county public library system, the concerns of zine librarians, despite the system and institution they work for, are surprisingly similar. While there is some overlap with previous zine librarian scholarship, Camper and Freedman did touch upon similar concerns for the future of zine librarianship and zine library collections.

In previous research, a focus is made upon the practical applications on forming zine collections rather than noting possible setbacks and struggles that zine librarians face in the midst of budget cuts, layoffs, and administrative hurdles. Revealed in the interviews with Camper and Freedman, the areas of concern for veteran zine librarians are whether or not zine libraries have the institutional buy-in of the parent library, strategic 'hit-by-a-bus' succession planning for existing zine library collections, and how zine librarians continue to build community amongst one another despite the distances between libraries.

## Institutional Buy-In

There has been a profound emphasis that zine library collections must have the full institutional and administrative support of its parent library. With collections as vulnerable as zine library collections, it is common that these fragile collections, along with their librarians, are the first subjected to inevitable budget cuts and layoffs. Freedman states, "If something has to get cut, [the zine library is] what is going to get cut" (Freedman, 2014, Interview). Even if the zine library has been in place for years, if the library administration does not believe in the role of zines filling the gap of alternative materials, the collection may perish.

When the parent library's administration understands the zine library to be a necessity, rather than an option to the greater library collection, both benefit. The zine library is allowed to exist within a large institution, which means stable housing for the collection with consistent funding. The larger library equally benefits as it represent materials beyond commercial catalogs and buying guides. In his essay on Jim Danky, Dilevko describes the act of collecting alternative materials as:

*...the responsibility of all librarians if they wanted to give full meaning to concepts such as equality, diversity, and substantive neutrality. If only mainstream publications were collected, Danky felt, substantive neutrality was impossible because, while such publications ventured to the left or the right of conventional wisdom on any given topic, they never went beyond a safe middle range of opinion that represented a consensus status quo* (Dilevko, 2008, 679-680).

Camper suggests pushing against the conventional boundaries, by placing onus and pressure upon librarians to become engaging, active participants in their library's collection development. The significance of ownership over alternative materials in collections may affect the way in which,

*Future researchers [who] will rely on materials like zines for*

*evidence of cultural dissent and innovation in the late twentieth century* (Dodge, 1995, 26).

If the institution makes little to no efforts in expanding the scope of its collection, then the collection will fail to remain relevant in the days ahead. Zines offer a window inside a sub-culture, and an insider view to alternative knowledge that is often too radicalized or counter cultural to be recognized by mainstream media outlets and publishers.

Most zine librarians are not hired to be zine librarians, but are retained as reference librarians, instructional librarians, outreach librarians, technical service librarians, etc. The zine librarian position comes part and parcel of the larger job description. This means that depending on how invested the library is of the zine library, zine librarians only are able to invest a small percentage of their employment into zines. A challenge that determines the amount of funding that parent libraries allocate for zine libraries, is proving that the worth of a zine library collection outweighs the cost of having and maintaining one (Camper, 2014, Interview). When the author inquired if being a zine librarian was Freedman's current role at the library, she responds:

> *Oh, how I wish it were... I have one day a week that I dedicate to librarianship. I catalogue zines from home [once a week], and then I do other zine librarianship things throughout the week as best as I can. Like supervising student workers, supervising visiting grad students, teaching a zine class, hosting a researcher, or responding to questions.* (Freedman, 2014, Interview).

Zines as a format, much like DVD/CD media, photographs, and databases require special attention to detail in the metadata and cataloging process. This original cataloging for unique items can be time-consuming for librarians, and place a cost-burden upon the library. While the original cataloging of zines allows increased accessibility for users, it can be a difficult to justify the costs.

Another issue institutions housing zine libraries must balance is what Woodbrook and Lazarro (2013) dub the "great tension" between the goals of preservation, and of access. Camper notes that for public libraries, the importance has shifted from a representative and permanent collection to a collection with a popular bent where circulation statistics is key to whether or not a zine is weeded or not.

> *For people doing research on Riot Grrrl or doing research on political activism or anarchy, they are going to look towards good collections that reflect that time period. For public libraries it is going to matter how popular zines are and how connected to the community the zinester or zine is* (Camper, 2014, Interview).

For public libraries, the emphasis is upon circulation and therefore on access. On the other hand, many academic and research zine libraries represent more of the archival preservationist mindset, where the focus is upon preserving cultural artifacts of the moment in the hopes that it will be of importance for future researchers. One of the reasons that Barnard Zine Library is unique is that it collects two copies of each zine, one for the now circulating zine library and one for the non-circulating zine archive.

Additionally, within the struggle for institutional buy-in, the issue arises of how to maintain the longevity of a zine library collection. In order for zine library collections to continue beyond one librarian's career span, the zine library must be the "library's project, not your project" (Freedman 2014, Interview). In order to ensure that the administration and library staff will take equal part ownership over the zine collection, they must see the zine collection as their own, not simply the project of a single librarian. The more library administration and staff are invested in the zine library, the more institutionalized the zine library becomes, and the longer the collection will hopefully be retained.

## "Hit by a Bus" Plans: Strategic and Effective Succession Planning

How can zine librarianship become more sustainable through back up plans, including both emergency contingency plans but also strategic succession planning? What if a situation happened that the main zine librarian could no longer be in charge of the zine library? Many zine libraries are initially founded by people passionate about zines, but through Camper and Freedman's interviews it has become clear that zine libraries are in trouble of failing if there isn't both institutional support coupled with effective knowledge transfer to successors.

Through a story of a special collection that was reliant upon a particular librarian, Camper tells the tale to highlight the need for effective knowledge transfer from the founding zine librarian to the new leadership.

> *When I was in Minneapolis, there was a librarian who was passionate about baseball. He created a huge database, and all these people that loved baseball were drawn in. But then he moved to a different department and it all dried up. Zine librarians are vulnerable to this because they usually come in with a passion for it, and they put in a lot of work, but can this work be passed on?* (Camper, 2014, Interview)

Effective strategic planning must have a component of active cultivation of leadership through avenues of mentorship, staff training, and the passing on of knowledge gained through experience. When the time comes to replace the original leadership, it is paramount that libraries are already in the process of developing key positions to manage and to retain the zine library (Singer and Griffin, 2010, 2). Cathy Camper notes that passing down knowledge increases the longevity of the zine library, encouraging the act of

> *...writing down what you do and [how] you are creating [the collection] as part of the job, and not just a personal thing* (Camper, 2014, Interview).

It is a charge for librarians who are concerned about the future of their collections, to begin the process of succession planning by investing in the next generation of zinester librarians. Within her work with the Women of Color Zine Collective of Portland, Oregon, and as an Outreach Librarian who teaches literacy classes with zines for Multnomah County Public Library, Camper constantly seeks ways to engage students in socially conscious conversations around zines, building community, and providing mentorship amongst zinesters through potlucks and gatherings.

For Camper, it was the love of zines that spurred her on to spearhead the zine library at Minneapolis Public Library. She explains that there was no one to question about the process in the early 1990s,

*There wasn't anybody to ask. It was more a feeling of: I love this. This needs to be collected. Let's do it. Versus now there is this generational [attitude] of 'Oh, there are other people that did it before me'* (Camper, 2014, Interview).

Camper's continued presence in the zine librarian community proves that she is a steady figurehead in Portland's zine community, but also known within zine and independent publishing circles outside of the PNW as well.

Camper's words heed a warning for zine librarians in that, the previous generations had little to no predecessors, and therefore had minimal guidance in the quest to forming zine libraries. While these librarians may have lacked guidance and support, they also had the freedom to form zine libraries as they saw fit. This was a open field day for zine librarians, and was a time to rely on colleagues to generate support, rather than relying on mentorships. These librarians had to be innovative and steadfast in their push for getting zines in libraries. They did not have a cushion of elder zine librarians to fall back upon.

The difference between the generational attitudes is important to point out. Zine librarians, in current times, have more robust resources, benefiting from the foundation that the previous generation formed and built upon. Resources, both online and in-person, like groups such as the Zine Librarianship list-serv, the Zine Pavilion planning team for the annual American Librarian Association conference, the Zine Librarians Facebook group, the annual Zine Librarians UnConference meet up, etc. The relationships that zine librarians form with each other is the bedrock of community building. It is what Camper calls "this island in the wilderness" and Freedman calls "her chosen family" (Camper and Freedman, 2014, Interview).

### Building Community Through Zine Networks

Both Freedman and Camper begin with their roles as community organizers as they outreach and interact to the people involved and interested in zines, self-publishing, and DIY culture. Camper defines the goal of labor within zine librarianship as a "community of people rather than a collection" (Camper, 2014, Interview). In fact both stress that a zine library is more than just a collection of publications but rather it's about the people that make and read zines, who invest in the zine community, who research and use zines in scholarship, who use zines as political tools, and as a way to organize community. Zines are a format that allow for critical thinking and dialogue; a format that encourages innovation and resistance. For Freedman, her daily life seeps into her zine librarianship and vice versa, as she is "an active part of the zine community...just a part of being a zine librarian about town"(Freedman, 2014, Interview).

For Camper, being a librarian is political, and she uses the opportunity in her zine workshops to teach students about race, class, sexuality and gender. Camper is actively subverting the narrative of who produces zines, and in term, presenting an increasingly more diversified and inclusive zine culture. Camper expounds on her experience:

> *Often I was doing the zine workshops for at-risk populations [and] for many kids of color. I couldn't do white zine curriculum like what the zine symposium was doing here in Portland. I needed to make it relevant or the students would say, "Who cares?"* (Camper, 2014, Interview).

Similarly, when asked how Barnard Zine Library came to collect zines by women of color, Freedman responds

> *I just felt it was important to go out of my way to collect zines by women of color. I can't say that I had this knowledge at the time, but the reason that I think it's so important is that there is such a narrative of white, middle class women in Riot Grrrl, and in zines. While it may be true that there was a majority of that profile, that doesn't mean there wasn't very active people of color or women of color communities in each of those groups. It seemed really important to document those groups (Freedman, 2014, Interview).*

Through the network of zine librarians, both interviewees note that being in community minimizes the risk for zine librarians giving up on their collections. There is a sense of accountability within the zine librarian network, so it is harder to just drop everything and leave.

> *[There are] those of us who are actively driving zine collections,*

*who make zines, really care about zines, so there is not the same ability to make promises to do something and then not do it, or get burnt out" (Freedman, 2014, Interview).*

It is valuable to note that without a strong community of support, zine librarians may begin to feel isolated and overwhelmed within their collections, thus forgetting that their issues are most likely similar to other zine librarians. This isolation may lead to burnout, and abandoning the well-intended beginnings of a zine library.

Yet, what will zine collections mean to people in the future? This will depend on if zines stay true to their original function: to provide an outlet for self-publishing, apart from the mainstream media and press, and to be a format of experimentation. It was Freedman who stated that she is

*...always looking a hundred years in the future, so what circulates now isn't maybe what is going to best serve people in another hundred years* (Freedman, 2014, Interview).

Her honest assessment of forming a zine collection is that as times change, the issues and concerns changes. Attitudes and interest shift throughout the decades. The way Freedman curates and collections rings true with Camper's attitude on the

*...level of importance that collecting zines has for the history of the underground movements in your locale. Because a lot of the times, nobody is collecting political zines or anarchist stuff, nobody is collecting that, and maybe that's exactly what people want to see fifty years from now"* (Camper, 2014, Interview).

## Conclusion

While the concerns in zine librarianship vary, the need for institutional buy in, succession plans, and continual community building efforts press down upon current zine librarians in both academic and public libraries. Zine librarians are individuals that have experience in fighting for the creation and establishment of zine libraries from where there was none before. It is in their initiative, innovation, determination, and resilience in maintaining working zine collections that inspire many aspiring librarians, especially those who are already into zines.

One of the limitations of this study was the small amount of people the author was able to interview. This limitation was due to the timeframe and limited financial resources of the study. The number of interviewees could increase in several ways: first, through short electronic surveys where a number of opinions could be gathered to compare against the more in-depth interviews. Secondly, more opinions could be gathered if the author was able to secure grant funding to attend the annual Zine Librarians UnConference. Many of the most active zine librarians are present at this gathering. Lastly, using the Zine Librarians Facebook group as a platform to conduct a poll or inquire a question or two. With an increased amount of surveying zine librarians, it would test the author's theories behind the issues and challenges that plague the current zine librarian job description.

Another limitation in this study is the technical complexity of the issues of metadata and the cataloging of zines. While this is an important issue for zines in libraries, because zines are an unique format treated unlike published books and periodicals, it is a topic matter based in technical services which is outside the range of the author's expertise. Freedman (2008) writes about creating original metadata for zines, as well as briefly addressing it in her interviews.

While this study did its best attempt from merely reiterating and regurgitating much of what is already written about in the literature, it does however begin to sound the alarm for zine librarians to begin creating emergency "hit by a bus" plans, participate in the active mentorship of future zine librarians, instill a sense of institutional pride and buy-in from within the parent library, while thinking forward on how to keep zine collections sustainably running even without its founder's passion, drive, and specialized knowledge.

Because zine collections are susceptible to budget cuts, it is important to have a well-developed succession and back up plan. Zine librarians should create shared workflows, detailed job descriptions, and enact active mentorship and internship opportunities to interested parties. When zine librarians are abandoned with the parent library not realizing the amount of dedication and specialized knowledge it takes to run a zine library, this ultimately may lead to the zine library's demise. The goal of this study is to prevent this decline in zine libraries. With preventative measures, zine libraries will be in good hands, and the next generation of zine librarians will be as resilience, socially conscious, and critically engaged as present day zine librarians.

# The Importance of Librarian Ethnic Caucuses and the Slander of "Self-Segregation"

## Jason Alston

## Abstract

With the seemingly-growing awareness and attention that the American Library Association and the profession of librarianship in general are now paying to diversity, some may question whether librarian ethnic caucuses and affiliates such as the Black Caucus of the American Library Association (BCALA) are still relevant and useful. Such organizations in librarianship formed to address specific ethnic constituencies could potentially be demeaned as "self-segregating," as this attempt at marginalization is frequently lodged at ethnic/racially-specific groups outside of librarianship. This chapter posits that BCALA and other ethnic caucuses still have relevance to the field and must continue on.

The author begins the chapter by explaining that people who oppose or do not understand the missions of groups founded to assist ethnic minorities have accused these groups of "self-segregation." The author then explains the focus/mission of some of these groups, and how this differs from racist segregation policies from America's past. The author then makes the argument that library ethnic caucuses are still beneficial today, and explains what these affiliates can offer that other library organizations and associations cannot. A case is then made as to why these organizations can be accepted as non-racist, but "white" organizations would be likely to have a racist initiative.

Before concluding the chapter, the author revisits the word "segregation," and explains why segregation is not an inherently harmful thing. Finally, the author concludes with a call to action for constituent ethnic minority practitioners to consider joining their constituent organizations.

They will demean it by calling it "self-segregation." U.S. Congressman Steve King (R-Iowa) did it; when criticizing the existence of the Congressional Black Caucus, King dismissed the legislative group tasked with recognizing and addressing the issues of Black Americans as a "self-segregating caucus" (Kaczynski, 2016). While not identifying the specific author of the quote, World Net Daily posed that "other commenters" (possibly including their own columnist, Jack Cashill) saw the formation of "White Student Union" groups on college campuses as, "a natural reaction to the sanctioned self-segregation" by collegiate organizations such as the Black Student Union, which are formed to help Black students identify and solve problems that they collectively face on campus (World Net Daily, 2015). A 2007 editorial in the Yale Daily News called out "cultural groups" such as Yale's Af-Am House and blamed them for "thwart(ing) campus unity" (Yale Daily News, 2007) through "self-segregation", prompting then-student Niko Bowie to pen a rebuttal calling "self-segregation" a myth (Bowie, 2007).

It is one of the many Catch-22s in contemporary discussions on race relations in the United States. Those who do not understand and/or do not care about the experiences and concerns of Blacks in America will be quick to tell Black Americans that we need to stop complaining about our plights, and the disadvantages that we face. They will tell us that we need to take responsibility for our own lives and pull ourselves up by our bootstraps in this great land of endless American opportunity. But, when we organize to attempt to solve our collective problems and take responsibility for ourselves and for each other, we are then maligned as self-segregators, as if our agenda is to exclude others from elevated opportunities that we feel we're exclusively entitled to. The nuance gets lost when the term "segregation" appears. The White supremacist segregation policies littering America's past were not aimed at bettering a population at a disadvantage; rather, they aimed to preserve a hierarchy and keep populations at a disadvantage. Today's Black organizations aim to destroy such historical disadvantages. But, there is so much weight to the term "segregation" that any entity described as "self-segregating" has no chance of appearing to have a benevolent goal.

Black organizations and caucuses such as the Congressional Black Caucus must be prepared to strike back at attempts to lazily equate them with the Whites-only institutions of the pre-Black Civil Rights Movement era. While the Congressional Black Caucus' record does include some unfortunate missteps, such as failure to maintain opposition to the Clinton Administration's devastating 1994 crime bill; it also has plenty of victories for Black Americans on its historical record, including convincing a reluctant President Richard Nixon to meet with Black legislators in the 1970s after he initially refused (Johnson, 2016). The Congressional Black Caucus also boasts of having helped organize Free South Africa Movement protests in the 1970s and 1980s to oppose apartheid (Johnson, 2016), and they continue to work with the nonprofit public policy and research institute, the Congressional Black Caucus Foundation (Congressional Black Caucus Foundation, Inc., 2017). Members of the Congressional Black Caucus were among the most vocal in January 2017 in opposing then-President-Elect Donald Trump's nomination of Senator Jeff Sessions for attorney general during Sessions' confirmation hearings (Tesfaye, 2017). From the moment the Congressional Black Caucus forced Nixon's hand all those years ago, the Congressional Black Caucus has maintained a mostly-positive record of attempting to combat racial hierarchies, not reinforce them.

The same can be said for other Black organizations that may be accused of "self-segregation", either publicly, or – more likely – via the disgruntled ramblings between those who just do not get it. Looking into the track records of organizations such as the National Black Graduate Student Association, the National Bar Association, the National Association of Black Social Workers, the National Association of Black Journalists, the National Society of Black Engineers, the National Association of Black Actors, and so on, will yield no history of attempting to elevate Black practitioners, Black students, or Black people in general to the top of a racial hierarchy. These groups all have similar aims to those stated by the National Association of Black Journalists. For the National Association of Black Journalists in particular, those stated aims include strengthening ties among Black professionals in their field, sensitizing the broader field to workplace fairness for Blacks, expanding job opportunities for Blacks in their field, and recruiting Blacks into their field (National Association of Black Journalists, u.d.). This is not Jim Crow-style exclusion. This is Black people organizing to ensure we enjoy inclusion and opportunity in the American dream. And it is taking responsibility for ourselves, which is what the right is insisting we do, right? These organizations are good for Black people, but their manifestation does not come at the expense of White or non-Black people. Their work is noble and must continue.

And similar work must continue in an organization that I hold life membership within: The Black Caucus of the American Library Association (BCALA). Founded in 1970, largely due to the efforts of the late Dr. E.J. Josey, the BCALA does not push an agenda among Black librarians to produce some sort of racial hierarchy that they would sit atop. Rather, BCALA was founded because Josey and others did not believe that the American Library Association, at the time, was addressing the needs and concerns of Black librarians and library workers (Black Caucus of the American Library Association, u.d.). Therefore, BCALA was formed to help Black library workers organize and improve their own lot: an exercise in taking initiative and taking responsibility for ourselves. BCALA's mission has evolved over time. Though not explicitly stated on the Caucus' web materials, BCALA maintains similar goals to those stated explicitly by the National Association of Black Journalists. BCALA is especially interested in ensuring that the broader profession is sensitive to the concerns and needs of Black practitioners and Black patrons and information seekers.

BCALA is also concerned with expanding job opportunities for Black practitioners and recruiting Blacks into the Library and Information Science (LIS) field. In 2016, BCALA held an informational meeting at historically-Black Florida A&M University's Law School to inform law students about opportunities they could have in the law field with both a masters in library science and a juris doctor (Simmons, 2016). Also, in addressing the concerns of Black library professionals and library users, it was BCALA that objected to the American Library Association (ALA) moving forward with plans to hold their annual conference in Orlando, Florida in 2016 in the wake of the acquittal of George Zimmerman in the fatal shooting of unarmed Black teenager Trayvon Martin.

## Should There Still Be a BCALA ?

Much has changed since the founding of BCALA. The ALA appears to have gained a cultural competence and concern for diversity in the workforce, diversity in collections, and diversity in programming. ALA now has an "Office of Diversity, Literacy & Outreach Services" that tasks itself with, "diversity, equity and inclusion" among other causes. ALA also has an active diversity committee, and there is an ALA roundtable – the Ethnic & Multicultural Information Exchange Round Table (EMIERT) – that speaks to concerns of multicultural diversity in the profession. ALA itself has also been headed by Black practitioners since the founding of BCALA. Clara Stanton Jones became ALA's first Black president in 1976, and since then, Black librarians E.J. Josey, Courtney Young, and Carla Hayden – who eventually became the first Black and first female librarian of congress – have also served as ALA presidents.

At least on its surface, the library profession in the 2010s established a decidedly leftist image, with practitioners often publicly championing the liberal viewpoints of issues related to diversity, equity, social justice, and inclusion. Contemporary librarians of all races and ethnicities appear to take to social media daily to let the whole world know that anti-racism is one of their most deeply-held and passionate convictions. While there are certainly practicing librarians who disagree with the prevailing hardline agenda for social justice, and certainly many others who are indifferent or tone-deaf to social justice concerns, their voices are drowned out by the louder, liberal-librarian contingent. So, with the library profession now more broadly concerned with diversity in general, and by virtue of this, Black practitioners and library users specifically, is there even any need for a BCALA? Is there also a need for the four other major ethnic librarian caucuses: REFORMA, the Chinese American Library Association, the Asian-Pacific Islander Library Association, and the American Indian Library Association? The original motivation for BCALA was that ALA was not looking out for the interests of Black librarians, but is this now no longer a concern? And, BCALA may have a present-day interest in recruiting Black practitioners of color and addressing the concerns of Black practitioners and Black library users, but aren't these issues also taken up by various other stakeholders in the library profession?

## Three Ethnic Caucus Advantages Identified by Dr. Robin Kurz

A concise yet viable statement that might prove useful when arguing to currently sustain BCALA actually came in the form of a tweet from Dr. Robin Kurz, a professor at Emporia State University's School of Library and Information Management. Kurz, a longtime member of REFORMA – the national association to promote library and information services to Latinos and the Spanish speaking – responded to a tweet from BCALA in which BCALA asked if those unsatisfied with an organization's direction attempt to change the organization from within, or if they end membership with the organization. While responding, Kurz said that ethnic caucuses such as REFORMA and BCALA offered greater control to members and featured less normalization of Whiteness than ALA; additionally, Kurz said that REFORMA is plagued with "far [less] institutional inertia" than ALA (Kurz, 2016). Kurz therefore identified three advantages offered to constituent populations by ethnic caucuses that ALA and other White-majority library organizations cannot provide: greater control of the organization by the organization's constituent population; limited/less normalization of Whiteness; and, reduced institutional inertia.

## Greater Control of the Organization

ALA has had Black presidents in the past; also, Loriene Roy was the first ever Native American president of ALA (American Indian Library Association, 2015), and Camila Alire was the first ever Hispanic president of ALA (McPherson, 2009). However, even with non-White individuals holding the ALA presidency at times, most of the leadership and general membership of ALA will be White, at least as long as the majority of the profession is White. Because of this, ALA will for the foreseeable future trend towards prioritizing the concerns of White librarians and LIS professionals. This is not to say that ALA will prioritize the prejudiced concerns of White librarians; instead, this is to entice one to ruminate on the future of librarianship for librarians of color when White professionals may lack the perspective that would allow them to recognize and fully appreciate the concerns of non-White practitioners. Librarians of color, and those particularly attuned to the concerns of library users of color, will need their own organizations; and, retaining full control of these organizations will allow them to prioritize their concerns.

In the behemoth that is ALA, the concerns of librarians or communities of color are likely to be addressed when the leadership of the association has time to address them, and in a manner that will likely be compromised in order to satisfy most of ALA's leadership. In an ethnic caucus like BCALA or REFORMA, such concerns can immediately rise to the forefront and be immediately and uncompromisingly addressed by organizational leadership. In addition, ownership of organizations gives librarians of color the ability to inspire and collaborate with other librarian groups from the outside. This advantage came into play during BCALA's objection to holding the 2016 ALA annual conference in Orlando, Florida. The Black librarians who stood with BCALA to oppose the decision to continue with holding the conference in Orlando were able to distribute a press release voicing their displeasure with the conference location and could directly speak to the greater librarian community without having to go through channels within ALA to be heard. And, the objection from BCALA did force a response from ALA, and, in turn, some concessions were made during the Orlando conference even though the conference proceeded in Orlando as planned.

## Limited/less Normalization of Whiteness

While it may seem poor form to cite what appears to be a troll comment in what is intended to be a serious write up, this particular troll comment does illustrate just how "normalized" Whiteness is in the library profession. When diversity-in-libraries advocate and MIT libraries director Chris Bourg penned a column entitled "The Unbearable Whiteness of Librarianship" on her personal blog in 2014, the first comment came from an individual presumably using a pseudonym (Bourg, 2014). Going by "Tom Krynicki," this commenter wrote:

> *"I am troubled by the under-representation of gay White men in the trash collection industry!! I am equally alarmed in the almost total lack of black representation as owners in the Chinese restaurant industry. OMG people, and here I thought librarians where [sic] supposed to be smart...... STOP!!"*

Normative Whiteness does not have a uniformly accepted definition, but can be generally understood as occurring when practices and policies position Whiteness as normative and categorizes all other things in relation to it (Gillborn, 2009). In the presumably trolling comment offered in response to Bourg's column addressing the underrepresentation of ethnic minorities in the American librarian workforce, "Tom Krynicki" offers an industry in which an ethnic normative would be appropriate. The Chinese restaurant industry profits from selling food items that are specific to Chinese culture and Chinese people. It would be appropriate, therefore, for Chinese people to have control, ownership and a normative position within the Chinese restaurant industry.

But what is "Tom Krynicki" getting at by comparing libraries to the Chinese restaurant industry in this fashion? Do White people have the same logical claim to ownership of the library industry that Chinese people have to the Chinese restaurant industry? Obviously, libraries are no place for racism or White normativity. The library is for use by all people, should contain diverse collections, and offer services that are relevant to diverse groups of people. The library's function should not have the end goal of serving a narrow market and generating profits for an administrative team whose societal contribution is sharing aspects of their specific culture. Practices within the Chinese restaurant industry actually should position being of Chinese descent and understanding Chinese culture and culinary techniques as normative. Practices and policies within libraries, however, should only "other" non-Whiteness when doing so aids access and/or usage (i.e. creating an "African-American section" that groups African-American materials together to make them easier to locate and browse).

The librarian ethnic caucuses offer less normalization of Whiteness than ALA and other librarian organizations by othering Whiteness itself. Within BCALA, it is actually "normal" to have a Black executive board, hold conferences where most of the attendees are Black, share information about Black literature, Black authors, and Black culture, and see images of Black librarians being normal librarians and Black library users doing normal library-user things. A White president of BCALA would be at least as striking and non-normative as a Black president of ALA, if not as striking as the confirmation of Dr. Carla Hayden to become the first Black Librarian of Congress in 2016. Within a society that is growing more diverse and a profession that claims to appreciate and promote diversity, there is a legitimate place for library organizations that can recognize the non-White as authentically normal. Because with "normal," comes comfort, safety and reduction of threats and fear. Organizations that can operate from a normative other than normative Whiteness can advise and influence the broader profession from a particularly informed position, because it is within these organizations that the most candid discussions and dialogues have occurred.

### Reduced Institutional Inertia

"Institutional inertia" occurs when institutions or organizations remain static and do not improve, change, or make progress even when circumstances may call for it (Olivos & Ochoa, 2008). The most obvious advantage of the ethnic caucuses is that they have smaller memberships than ALA and, therefore, fewer voices to consider and reason with. The ethnic caucuses also tend to be more homogenous than ALA, and the inherent similarity of culture and perspective can potentially reduce internal conflicts and disagreement as organizational members strive to find unity of purpose. ALA remains accountable to a host of stakeholders inside and outside of the actual library field and positions itself as a highly influential national organization. In contrast, the ethnic caucuses avoid being laden with accountability to so many stakeholders by positioning themselves as organizations with a specialized mission and purpose. When Donald Trump won the 2016 presidential election through what many felt was a divisive campaign exploiting misogyny and White nationalism, ALA issued – then quickly backtracked – press releases expressing its desire to work with the new administration; this prompted a lot of pushback from practicing librarians (Litwin, 2016), but ALA likely considers the federal government a stakeholder to which they feel some accountability. The ethnic caucuses, however, did not feel beholden to any federal administration in this way, and did not express any desire to work with or support the Trump administration.

*Additional Professional Development Opportunities*

The three advantages identified by Kurz for the existence of REFORMA, BCALA and the other ethnic caucuses do encompass the most important reasons for these organizations to still exist. However, it should also be noted that these organizations (like most library organizations) generally offer L.I.S. professionals increased chances to publish, present, share ideas, and take advantage of professional development. For example, BCALA publishes a quarterly publication that gives librarians an added venue to increase the number of publications on their VITA. BCALA also holds a conference where professionals seeking tenure can elect to present, and where professionals needing new ideas and exposure to new concepts can go to learn and network. Given the interdisciplinary nature of the field of librarianship, it is advantageous for there to be as many venues for publishing, presenting and networking as possible. The ethnic caucuses also specifically provide publication and presenting opportunities for ideas and items that other venues find irrelevant or not important enough.

*But a W.C.ALA Would Be Racist!*

Inevitably, whenever you have an organization formed by Black people to primarily serve the needs of Black people, there are those who insist that an organization formed by White people to primarily serve the needs of White people would be racist. Perhaps due to the current social justice mood of the librarian profession in 2017, those who feel this way about organizations serving a particular race by design do not voice their objections in social media or other public forums. However, it may be naïve to think that just because these rumblings are not heard publicly, that they are not happening; similar rumblings are occurring wherever else you find organizations that focus on assisting Black people by design. It might prove useful to focus on the motivations under which the organization was founded. To reiterate, BCALA was originally formed because Dr. E.J. Josey and others did not believe ALA was representing the needs of Black librarians. BCALA continues today in an effort to support Black librarians and Black library users, as well as address any inequities that Black librarians and Black library users may encounter. BCALA's objective is not to place its constituent population atop any racial hierarchy.

For Black Americans specifically, some collective concerns include erasing the gap in educational achievement between Black and White students, addressing crime and poverty in Black-majority communities, addressing higher rates of obesity, diabetes, heart disease, cancer, and HIV/AIDS, and other issues. Black people can organize and mobilize to work towards solving these issues together without their objectives being anti-White, or against any other race or ethnicity. "White issues" tend to not be clearly or specifically defined; and when someone speaks about "White issues", they tend to be promoting pushback against other ethnicities. White people as a collective are not largely concerned with erasing any educational achievement gaps between them and another ethnicity; for instance. A "White issue", if brought up explicitly, would more likely consist of conserving the White majority and Anglo identity of the United States, perhaps by doing things such as curbing (non-White) immigration. BCALA and its membership can articulate actual concerns for Black librarians and Black library users in particular that require specific attention. And these concerns are not concerns rooted in opposing other ethnic groups. If a White Caucus of the American Library Association (WCALA) could articulate actual concerns for White librarians and White library users in particular that require specific attention, and these concerns were not rooted in preserving a racial hierarchy or opposing other ethnic groups, the WCALA's purpose could be viewed as benevolent and non-racist. But, so far, no one has come forward to present such a WCALA.

### Revisiting the term "Segregation"

Without the "self-segregating" presence of BCALA, Black librarians and Black library users would be at the mercy of ALA, and other predominantly-White library organizations to hopefully acknowledge and help address their concerns. And, these library organizations may or may not choose to be receptive, which would leave Black librarians and library users in the same predicament they were in before Josey founded BCALA. There is power in a contingent that voices its concerns, and BCALA allows for those concerns to manifest. Merriam-Webster defines segregation as "the art or process of segregating," and defines "segregate" as, "to separate or set apart from others or from the general mass." An added definition for segregation is, "the separation for special treatment or observation of individuals or items from a larger group." What groups like BCALA do could fit either definition; BCALA does, indeed, allow for Black librarians to be set apart from the general mass of librarians, 88% of whom were non-Hispanic White according to 2009-2010 figures (American Library Association, 2012).

However, because Black librarians control BCALA, they are empowered to push through initiatives and agendas within BCALA that they may not have the numbers to push through within organizations with demographics more closely reflecting the profession's 88% White population. BCALA also allows for, "separation for special treatment or observation of individuals from a larger group," in some respects. The idea of "special treatment" may bother some, but special treatment does not necessarily result in an elevated status in a hierarchy; any special treatment that a group like BCALA may offer may merely be what it takes to ensure previously-unheard voices are acknowledged. Also, the actual degree of "segregating" due to BCALA or the other ethnic caucuses is minimal. BCALA members work in a profession that is 88% White, a profession that is actually Whiter than the broad population of the United States of America. Many BCALA members devote very little of their professional time to BCALA and the overwhelming majority of their time to institutions that are staffed mostly by White practitioners.

BCALA also does not consider itself a space for only Black practitioners; BCALA is a space for allies as well. While there are some arenas where allies of traditionally disenfranchised populations are asked to respect the space and not enter it, BCALA is not such a place. And, BCALA has White members and members of many other ethnicities, as do all of the ethnic caucuses. It's probably possible to truly segregate oneself from White people in the library profession, but it would be quite an accomplishment. As discussed earlier, one go-to tactic for those who wish to delegitimize groups like BCALA is to write them off as examples of Black self-segregation. The response should not be to attempt to say that BCALA and similar organizations do not actually self-segregate. The appropriate response is to explain what "segregation" as a word actually means, and then to explain that not all segregation holds the goal of creating or preserving racial hierarchies.

## Conclusion: A Call to Action

BCALA and the other ethnic caucuses are noble organizations with noble purposes. However, in order for them to reach their full potential, their constituent populations have to engage them, hopefully join them, and, in some manner, become active within them. The ethnic caucuses, like all other library organizations and I'd presume all professional organizations, have their flaws. I have heard just as many complaints about BCALA over the years as I have compliments. But to Black practitioners, BCALA is small enough that increased participation from Black practitioners can change it for the better; changing BCALA would not be as daunting a task as changing ALA. But, even with its flaws, and even with the difficulties that we have working together with each other as Black librarians, I still recognize BCALA as our best avenue to ensure we can influence this profession, our profession. I would also suggest that Black practitioners not over-extend themselves in BCALA; I believe that those who burn out on the organization are those who, with good intentions, get too involved with the Black Caucus and get frustrated by its institutional problems. Being an active BCALA member may mean just being involved with one committee or taking on some volunteer work for the caucus. Do not give the Caucus more than you can without compromising your sanity.

Figure 5

# I'm Not A Token: Reflections on Black and Latinx Representation and Youth Services

Diana Lopez and Aquita Winslow

Why is diversity in librarianship so important? This is a very basic question, but a very important one. When we think of the value of the resource that is the "library," we must ask ourselves who benefits the most from this resource? Most libraries in this country are extensions of educational institutions, primary, secondary, undergraduate, and graduate schools. Even our public libraries are often bridging the gap between educational resources in public schools, and community resources available for lifelong learning, and are therefore educational establishments at their core. While libraries have been evolving in this new century to be centers of community, the function of librarians--to help support learning, research and reading-- has remained constant. If Libraries are meant to be at the heart of learning, then librarians are by necessity the core of student learning.

For students of color, this is particularly important. Many students of color do not feel that schools support or even want them. In their article, "The Success of African-American Students in Independent Schools," the National Association of Independent Schools (N.A.I.S.) points out that 70% of African American students in the study believed it was hard for people like them to be accepted at their independent schools, and 62% of the same students did not feel like the belonged in their school (Arrington, Hall, & Stevenson, 2003, p. 2). In addition, many students of color in our public school systems are experiencing the Pushout phenomenon. In her book "Pushout: The Criminalization of Black Girls in Schools," author Monique Morris points out that schools have increasingly become places that isolate and discourage young black girls from education. Morris writes, "One of the most persistent and salient traits among girls who have been labeled delinquent is that they have failed to establish a meaningful and sustainable connection with schools. This missing link is exacerbated by the increased reliance of public school on exclusionary discipline, at present one of the most widely used measures to deal with problematic student behaviors" (Morris, 2016, p.3).

If we want to support students of color, we need diverse voices that they can trust--voices from people who look like them and voices from their communities, at their churches, in the grocery stores, and in their schools. We need diversity in public and school libraries because without diversity, libraries become like schools: places where students of color do not feel wanted or supported. Librarians (public, private, school, and university) have a responsibility to cultivate impressionable relationships with our patrons. These relationships have lasting effects. Many students find that libraries and librarians are harsh and do not create a feeling of welcome. This lack of welcome is very important.

The difference between a classroom teacher's connection with a student and a librarian's connection is patrons choice. Students have to interact, listen to and connect with teachers/professors. Students are graded by teachers/professors, and therefore have a vested interest in connecting positively with teachers. Students do not have to engage in meaningful relationships with librarians. Students can choose to connect with us or not, and we will still provide service to them. This distinction is important because it shows that we have a burden our fellow teachers do not have. The lure of the internet has lead many students to believe that they do not need libraries. This revelation has propelled libraries to change how we interact with our patron, so that we can prove to students that the library as a place is still relevant to their lives.

Librarians of color should understand that one of their roles is to make their library a safe space for other students of color. For example, when I was a child, I spent all my time in the library. The library was my safe space. I was lucky to have librarians that not only fostered my love of reading but made the library a space where a young African American girl felt welcome. Unfortunately, not enough of our youth have this same introduction to libraries. However, as my career has progressed I have learned that that is only a small part of my role as a librarian. My real job is to make all my students see the value of libraries in their lives because adults who have positive library experiences as children become lifelong library users.

## Student/Youth Impact: Diana

I grew up in Glendora, California, a small city about 20 miles east of downtown Los Angeles. The town was predominately white when I attended Glendora Unified School District schools. Back then, I think, there were maybe two or three Latino students, one African-American student, and a couple of Asian students. I remember going into the downtown shops in the Glendora Village, many of which were owned by middle-aged or elderly white women, and being watched as if they could not trust the little Mexican girl not to steal something. Little did they know that my grandfather was a retired Glendora Police Captain, and I would have been in unimaginable trouble if I had stolen anything (not that I wanted to anyway). I think that because the library was next to the police station, I was there all the time as a child. Despite this, the library did not feel like it was truly my home. Los Angeles is well known for having a diverse population, but my experiences only a short distance away were more isolating. The lack of diversity and the community played a role in making me feel isolated, but so did the books available to me and the library's staff.

My grandfather was an avid reader, and the reason why I came to love reading as well. But as much as I loved my local library, I cannot recall it ever being staffed by anyone who looked like me. Nor did I read books that included characters that shared my heritage. This is similar to writer Zetta Elliott's experience. In her guest blog post entitled "Book Smarts" on the Public Libraries blog, Zetta Elliott talks about a familiar experience that many of us have had and one that we will perpetuate without diversity in the library field and in our collections: she had not been assigned to read any books by authors of color until her last semester of college. This troubling realization made her conclude that, "I had been erasing myself when I read," she says (Book Smarts, 2016, par.1).

I stumbled into the library profession quite by accident when I accepted a temporary assignment at a high school library. I loved it! Before that, I did not know that librarianship could have been a career path for me. From there, I decided to look for full-time, permanent work in a library. I was hired to run a middle school library, which I did for a year and then because I needed a 12-month position, I took a job at a community college library. During all of this, I decided to obtain my library technology certificate to see if I liked studying the field before I dove into an MLIS program. Throughout, I kept having recurring "light-bulb" moments and realized that this was where I should have been all along. But, again, not having ever seen a Latina librarian or Mexican kids in the books that I was reading, it never entered my realm of possibilities that I could do this. And so, it is for many of us in the library field, and why we must address the lack of librarians of color.

This lack of diversity in librarianship was discussed in the Association of Library Services to Children's ("ALSC 2016 Environmental Scan"). One of the sections directly addresses some of the problems caused by the lack of diversity in librarianship. A public library children's services manager acknowledges that many of us already know: "We need MANY more librarians of color in our profession. It is disheartening to see the great need children of color have for representations in books, then also mirrored in the people that help them select books" ("ALSC 2016 Environmental Scan"). The lack of racial diversity in our field is a self-perpetuating cycle: Because children are not seeing librarians of color, they do not see them as role models in positions that they can aspire to. "If children of all backgrounds only see the library profession as [a profession] for white people, then the likelihood that children of color and Native/First Nations children will enter the profession is reduced". ("ALSC 2016 Environmental Scan").

The scarcity of librarians of color also affects the creation of library programs, collection management, and even the patrons' impression of the library. "When students or library users do not see themselves represented in library staff, they may find it difficult to approach librarians for assistance" (Stanley 83). Stanley was referring to academic libraries, but this easily translates to all library environments. For those of us who are librarians of color have certainly had the experience of patrons with a shared ethnicity responding to them with an understood connection and approaching them first rather than the white colleague sitting next to them. As Stanley points out, "there are many things white librarians can, and should, do to support the diverse communities they serve, but the input and presence of a diverse group of librarians is essential to the profession and to serving all communities with the excellence they deserve."

According to the Department for Professional Employees, AFL-CIO's Library Workers Facts & Figures fact sheet, there were 166,000 librarians in 2015. Of those librarians, about 84% were predominantly non-Hispanic Whites, only 8.5% of librarians were Black or African American, 4.8% were Hispanic or Latino, and 2.8% were Asian. For the purposes of this chapter, diversity refers to ethnicity and race, but to be sure, diversity can also include people with various abilities, sexual orientations and identities. For example, the "ALSC 2016 Environmental Scan" states:

> *If the library becomes a place where all children feel welcomed, and that their culture is being honored and celebrated, then the likelihood that children from traditionally underserved groups will consider librarianship increases. Since the overwhelming majority of librarians are white, this diversity is essential. As the field of children's librarianship diversifies, it naturally follows that collections, programming, and library spaces themselves will become ever increasingly welcoming and supportive spaces for people who have been traditionally underrepresented by the library field and possibly underserved by libraries. Ultimately, in order to serve all young people, diversity must be considered in all aspects of children's librarianship. Diversity must be an integral part of the field, as opposed to a separate, "special" topic (ALSC, 2016).*

In her book "Pushout: The Criminalization of Black Girls in School," Monique W. Morris discusses the academic performance of Black students being directly linked to their relationships with their teachers, "which may be problematic given that Black children are often labeled as "less conforming and more active" than their white counterparts, resulting in interactions with teachers that are "characterized by more criticism and less support" (Morris 38). Clearly, not having teachers, including teacher-librarians that represent the student demographics has a negative impact on children. Students want and need to have people who look like them. As my colleague Aquita Winslow pointed out below, if we are going to properly support our children of color, we need diverse faces and voices in our libraries to welcome and understand them. ALSC warns us that "in terms of the atmosphere, school librarians should be sensitive to the fact that many youth of color feel like outsiders in library spaces and deem the school library as sole "property" of the librarian" ("ALSC 2016 Environmental Scan"). This is an especially crucial time to note this as Latino children alone are projected to be 39% of all the children in the United States by 2050 ("Public Library Services and Latino Children," pg. 38).

Tatum points out the ameliorative benefits of including multicultural literature in our collections: "…by providing children of color with positive cultural images and messages about their race, parents and caregivers not only encourage positive racial identity development but also mitigate the impact of stereotypes" (as cited in Hughes-Hassell and Cox 212). Including multicultural children's books in our collections should not depend solely on the demographics of the community served by the library. Demographics may vary (even within library systems), but [what must be recognized]…is that children are living and growing up in a diverse world, and it is important that they learn about the people and cultures around them ("ALSC, 2016 Environmental Scan"). I would stress that cultural competency should be—if not addressed in library school—a part of the onboarding of any new library staff. This would benefit patrons and colleagues as well—especially if a system is lacking in diversity among the staff. "Cultural competency is a developmental process that evolves over an extended period and refers to an ability to understand the needs of diverse populations and to interact effectively with people from different cultures" ("Librarians Working with Diverse Populations", 2010). Mestre goes on to say:

> *"Whereas there are often diversity training sessions for individuals to learn how to become culturally aware and sensitive to others, training to be culturally competent extends beyond that. One must also be trained to recognize the various learning and communication styles of others and to be able to adjust one's habits based on those style differences in order to best interact with cultures other than one's own ("Librarians Working with Diverse Populations", 2010).*

In my library field experience, I have directly experienced a stark lack of cultural competency among my white colleagues. Like the colleague Ms. Winslow discussed below, I too have faced microaggressions and some blatant racism intertwined with sexism in my career. Microaggressions are subtle insults (verbal, nonverbal, and/or visual) directed toward people of color, often automatically or unconsciously" (Alabi 2014). Alabi defines colorblindness as "professing not to see another's race" and "an example of a microinvalidation because it denies the experiential reality of people of color who are treated differently because of their race"

(Alabi 2014). In addition to presenting a classification scheme for racial microaggressions, Sue, Capodilupo, et al. (2007) also note that the subtle nature of microaggressions makes them particularly difficult to defend against. For example, a single microaggression can often be dismissed as a misunderstanding or rationalized with a non-racist explanation, which can make identifying a microaggression challenging.

Even when a person of color determines that a microaggression has occurred, she may be trapped in a no-win situation—if she responds, she will expend energy educating someone who may respond defensively; if she does not respond, she may feel anger and guilt at herself or internalize the microaggression (Alabi 2014). If allowed to continue in this no-win situation, librarians of color will not stay in their positions; the expectation for us is to not upset the apple cart that is white fragility which creates an adverse and very stressful environment.

> *"White Fragility is a state in which even a minimum amount of racial stress becomes intolerable, triggering a range of defensive moves. These moves include the outward display of emotions such as anger, fear, and guilt, and behaviors such as argumentation, silence, and leaving the stress-inducing situation. These behaviors, in turn, function to reinstate white racial equilibrium. Racial stress results from an interruption to what is racially familiar"* (Di Angelo 2011).

The situation is compounded for women of color. "While sexism shapes the nature of womanhood, white womanhood looks very different than Asian-American, Black, Indigenous, or Latina womanhood, because each woman's experience is shaped by the internal expectations and external perceptions of what it means to be a woman within each of these racial communities" (Accapadi 2007).

With each library position that I have had, I have experienced microaggressions, sexism, and have been either the only librarian of color with an MLIS or one of two (and the only one in public service with supervisorial responsibilities). I will share the most glaring examples.

Examples from my own experience include:

- When I was a paraprofessional in library school, a white male and recent MLIS graduate joined our staff as a librarian and my supervisor. He micromanaged me even though I had been there for years and had been working independently. He also told me that I was "opinionated" and that I had a "strong personality." When my white male colleague expressed himself, it was accepted—even if we shared the same opinion.

• When I first started my position, I noticed a huge lack of diversity in our children's collection. I immediately voiced this, and was often met with silence and an uncomfortable atmosphere in the room. Regardless, I have fought to increase the diversity in the collection, because I believe that children should see themselves and be exposed to other cultures and experiences (cultural, racial, aptitudes, etc.).

• I am seen as a paraprofessional without being acknowledged as a librarian in a professional position that requires an MLIS.

• A white, female supervisor has twice included herself when it came time to have publicity for a successful partnership and program that I spear-headed—something that she had nothing to do with. Both of these occurrences left me feeling marginalized. The first time that I attempted to discuss my feelings with her, she was surprised that I felt that way and then turned the conversation into being about her by saying, "I don't want to feel like I can't walk through the door." I did not say anything like that, and not only was her comment hyperbolic, it was also full of white privilege. I spoke with her again and gave her a copy of Mamta Motwani Accapadi's article "When White Women Cry: How White Women's Tears Oppress Women of Color." My manager and I have not spoken again about the article or the events that transpired yet it feels to me like an elephant in the room.

• A female white colleague talked to a library assistant on my staff—a direct report to me—and without asking me first, went to our supervisor to ask about adding a new subscription mid-fiscal year to a youth magazine. The supervisor responded by saying that she would ask our Friends group to fund the subscription and contact our Technical Services Department to add the subscription.

When I spoke up, our supervisor said she was merely moving the conversation along, and my colleague said that she felt she did not deserve "the spank" that she was getting from me. I emailed a response saying to both of them that it was hard enough to be a librarian of color in our system. My supervisor did not respond to my email saying that the language in her email indicated that she was moving forward with the subscription. No mention of this has been made since.

All in all, the feelings of marginalization and "otherness" have really made me want to move on from my current position. My Library Director is very vocal about appreciating my efforts and having respect for me professionally. My staff and my patrons appreciate me as well. I believe and have been told by many that I have made a difference in the community I serve, yet I feel that I want to do more, and THAT is what keeps me in my position.

So, what can we do to improve diversity in our field, even if some of our workplaces continue to hire more whites? The topics of recruitment and retention are key here. As Ortega and Ramos point out, "the issue of recruiting minorities into the information science field is not a new one and has been addressed by its professional organizations since the 1970s" (Pathways to Progress pg 103). Affiliate groups like the Black Caucus, Chinese American Librarians Association (CALA), and REFORMA were established "in response to a perceived lack of support inside the ALA in dealing with the many issues affecting underrepresented librarians and users" (Ortega). While efforts such as those by REFORMA, ALA's Spectrum recruitment and scholarship, grant programs from the Institute of Museum and Library Services and library schools have been implemented, we are clearly still lacking in diversity in our field. To get at the root of the problem, we need to start early and look at high school graduation rates. For example, in 2000 Hispanic students were 13.5% of the total population according to the U.S. Census, but they were only 7% of college students. Furthermore, they have a higher dropout rate compared to other ethnic and racial groups. The 2008 rate dropout rate was "18% for Hispanic Americans compared to 9.9% for African American, 14.6% for Native American, 4.4% for Asian/Pacific Islander, and 4.8% for whites" (Ortega). If not enough Hispanics are graduating from high school, it would follow that they are not enrolling in college towards Bachelor's degrees, let alone MLS programs.

Ortega and Ramos conclude that this pipeline problem is a main factor in the lack of Hispanic Americans in the library field. "Not enough Hispanics are entering four-year colleges, and many of them may choose to go to community colleges or HSI (Hispanic serving institutions) colleges to acquire a degree that would lead them to the workforce as soon as possible. Therefore, they may not consider a master's degree in library science as a choice, either because of economic reasons or because they were never made aware of such a career option (Ortega). Ortega and Ramos offer some excellent suggestions for recruiting more people Latinxs into our field including:

> • At the college level, collaborative projects between library staff, career counselors, and staff at cultural centers can reach and mentor students

> • Student workers in libraries can also be recruited and mentored

> • Outreach to students from ethnic studies programs like Chicano, Puerto Rican, Latino, and Latin American Studies (The same would hold true for outreach to African-American and Asian Studies programs.)

> • Start early with junior high and high school students

> • Target paraprofessionals of color who are already working in our libraries (Ortega).

## Mentorship: Aquita.

I recall my first job interview out of library school. I was 23, fresh out of graduate school, and excited at the prospect of my first professional library job. I interviewed with an agency that specialized in private business libraries in San Francisco. The man who interviewed me was surprised at my appearance when I walked through the door. My name and my voice do not belie my race. While looking at my resume, this man said to me, "Well, the last person who had this job had a Master's degree in Library

Science." At this point, I smiled and said I had a Master's degree in Library Science!  The interviewer looked at me with shock and said, "From a four year institution?" While I would like to say that this type of blatant bigotry only happened to me once in my career, I came to realize that this was the norm. I would always have to prove my value and my worth. No matter how exceptional my resume, or how stellar my references, when I walked in the door, I would always be black first and librarian second. Librarians of color all over the country have dealt with subtle and blatant bigotries through the span of our careers. As librarians, we see ourselves as educators, bastions of free speech, and the champions of access to information, but that does not preclude us from also being racist or biased or bigoted.

Studies show that racism has not decreased in this country, but is more disguised and covert rather than overtly expressed in the form of racial hatred and bigotry (Sue, 2010, p.23). While the library ethos is inclusiveness, our statistics show otherwise. 88% of all librarians in this country are white, specifically white women (Diversity Counts, 2012, p.1). We believe in inclusiveness but not in an inclusive array of colleagues? With only 12% of the entire profession comprised of people of color, I think the statistics speak for themselves. We need librarians of color to actively support our ever growing patron base of color. Librarian Cheylon Woods makes this point very succinctly in her response to the article: "MLS and the Race Line:"

> *Racial/ ethnic diversity is important in the library workforce because you are missing an entire portion of your patron base... You will always struggle to understand the underlying needs of these patrons because they will rarely open up to you. People who feel that the system has oppressed them do not trust the system, and libraries are a part of the system. Regardless if you were there or not, there is a history of segregation and exclusion in the history of librarianship. Entire communities were not allowed to enter libraries, and their stories were deemed too insignificant to collect. As a survival technique, these now underserved patrons learned to lean on themselves and their communities to fulfill their information needs...They will trust someone who looks like them much more than they will trust you, there is an almost instant*

*connection because there is a kinship that you can never establish. Why do you need minorities in libraries? You don't. Your patrons do. Why do you need, minorities in your archives as archivists? Because we can get the collections that you can't. We can build a relationship that you will never be able to establish. We can get the stories from our people that they will never tell you. That is why you need us (Kelley, 2013).*

Librarians of color are entering the profession with a steep learning curve ahead of them, and they don't even know it. While many new librarians understand that they need to prove themselves professionally, many don't realize they also have to prove themselves racially. What does this mean? Librarians of color need to prove that they can withstand the stress, the isolation, the anger and resentment that they will most certainly feel as a minority in a position of authority at an institution. The constant questions to test our competence; the open and verbal surprise upon promotion; the tacit expectation that it is our job (not theirs), to make white peers feel comfortable with a person of color in an equal or superior position: these unspoken job requirements are often the reason that librarians of color leave their positions, or leave the profession altogether. And, while those of us who stick it out figure out how to deal with the microaggressions that are part and parcel of our profession, many of the issues that librarians of color face could be alleviated with supportive mentorship.

Research clearly states that people of color fare significantly better in organizational hierarchy when they are mentored (Thomas 2015). Mentorship is not just about training. It is about acceptance into situations and organizations that were not made for people of color, and where, if left alone, people of color will not succeed. Thomas points out that many organizations do not view people of color in the same way they view whites. Thomas notes, "This is evident by the fast tracking of some white professionals to executive roles." He points out that people of color in these same situations are often not seen as executive until they have been tested and proven trustworthy. This process of vetting people of color often diminishes or extinguishes our desire to work for an organization or stay in a profession. Librarians of color who have positive mentors often do feel as if they are being tested. Mentors fulfill some very important functions for professionals of color. Mentors act as coaches, counselors, and advocates. A mentor can teach a librarian of color the ins and outs of an organization so that they can progress quicker. They can be a sounding board when there is a problem, and they can smooth the way before the librarian even begins working by saying and doing thing that show the rest of the staff that this person is to be heeded, and respected. Finally, mentors can help librarians with networking and creating additional professional relationships that are crucial to a person's long-term success.

This relationship does need to take into account race. Since 88% of our profession is white, many of our mentors will be white as well. Cross-race mentoring can be successful, but each member of the partnership must respect some specific ground rules. Mentors must understand that for librarians of color race is always an issue and we need to be able to talk openly about our struggles with race at work. I remember when I worked as a children's librarian for a city library district in Southern California. I had a wonderful boss. She was kind and understanding. I enjoyed the environment she created in the branch, and she gave good advice. Once, I came to her with a frustration: I had noticed that suburban white mothers who came into the children's room would not ask me for help. For me, this was not something new. When I was in graduate school, I worked for a law firm as a library intern. None of the lawyers would talk to me. If I was the only one in the library, lawyers and paralegals would leave and come back later. In my current position, I would watch the mothers come in and look for anyone to help them but me. I would watch them go to the circulation desk only to be directed to my desk for reference services, and once at my desk, they would ask "Are you the Librarian?......I mean the real librarian?"

After several weeks of this, I spoke to my boss and asked what I could do. I expressed to her that it made me very uncomfortable and that I felt it was racial in nature. My boss was not equipped for this question, having never had a librarian of color in her branch before. Her advice was to be perky and head off their apprehension before it could develop. Her advice did not speak to my issues. Rather, she tried to focus on helping the patron instead of helping me. If a librarian is going to mentor across racial lines, she must be open to questions that she cannot answer because they might be racial in nature. Whether it be stereotypes about language, peer behavior, or issues of racial, bias, mentors must possess the cultural competency to listen and as Thomas states "Give the person of color the benefit of the doubt." Leaving space to talk openly about race does not mean that we are automatically right in what we say or how we feel. What is essential is knowing that we can speak our truth without automatically being wrong or losing our job, or possibly foregoing advancement. In the article "Mentoring Minority Graduate Students: Issues and Strategies for Institutions, Faculty, and Students," the authors illustrate the above point.

> *Given minority students' historical exclusion from institutions of higher education, the persistent group stereotypes that relate to their academic abilities and competencies as well as their unique cultural perspectives demand that more attention needs to be paid to the qualities needed to effectively mentor this group. For example, good mentors are knowledgeable and sensitive to the issues their students face. To mentor minority graduate student protégés, mentors knowledge could be expanded to include the day-to-day experiences of being a racial minority on their campus as well as mentor's cultural competence (Thomas, Willis, & Davis, 2007, p.181).*

Being a good mentor requires a set of skills many members of our profession have not been trained to possess. In this list I include librarians and school and university administrators as well.

Many mentors do not factor in the challenges that race plays in circumstances and how race impacts virtually every aspect of our jobs. For example, most librarians of color know that they have to walk a very fine line when it comes to expressing anger. When our white colleagues become angry, either at a situation or at us, we are expected to accept their anger, and there is relatively never a consequence for their expressions of anger. However, if a person of color expresses anger in the same way, they are labeled; they can be labeled an "angry black man" or "angry black women." Furthermore, when your anger subsides you are still held accountable for the initial action for years to come. For example, "Oh, don't get her angry. You'll never hear the end of it," or constant check-ins to make sure that you will not have another "outburst." These microaggressions can create an environment where people of color can feel even more isolated and unwilling to express themselves. Mentors of color can help teach mentee's how to express anger and frustration in ways that don't create negative labeling or pushback. As people of color, we have different rules in the workforce and society. Mentors must listen to their mentee's and accept their reality.

Many professionals of color do feel their ideas are ignored or that they are simply ignored in meetings. This can be a particular problem for librarians whose first language is not English. For example, a colleague at my work who is from Spain is often frustrated that she will say something in a meeting and no one will respond. Later in the conversation, a white male colleague will say the same thing, and everyone will respond and credit him with a brilliant idea. This type of behavior leaves a professional of color feeling invisible and creates a great deal of resentment that she is not getting credit for her contributions to the collective. Mentors must listen to the experiences of people of color and not dismiss them, or play them down due to discomfort. Mentors have to be ready to lean into discomfort with mentoring professionals of color. Mentors must take the coaching and counseling aspects of their role very seriously. Sometimes, the difference between a small situation resolving amicably and a small situation becoming a large problem is the ability of the person in the mentoring/supervising role not jumping to conclusions, and remaining supportive.

What you do behind the scenes is not simply about the relationship you foster with your mentees, it is about how you support and promote them in other circles. Let us not forget that peer mentors and colleagues are taking their cue on how to treat their colleagues of color from their supervisors and mentors, and possibly their detractors. It is imperative that mentors use every opportunity, conversation, and possible occasion to actually promote and support a mentee. This could look like praising a mentee for a job well done, talking about their good nature, or as simple as giving them credit for their ideas and suggestions. Finally, being constant with equal treatment across the board in problem situations is also essential to a mentee's success. It is important to note that the latter activities may never be known by your mentee's if done correctly. These types of activities will become standard practice for people of color as well, and their comfort level and trust level will increase as a result.

Mentors must not shy away from the discomfort of race or bias that they may feel personally; mentors need to not shy away from the discomfort of speaking about race. The goal for cross-cultural mentors is not to act as if race does not exist. However, when we do not address our own biases, people of color enviably suffer. No one is comfortable in these situations, but skirting the issue can lead to librarians of color leaving their positions. For instance, one of the hardest times I weathered, professionally, was being an administrator/library director for a prominent high school. I learned early in my tenure at this high school that white women did not like being supervised by a Black woman. I watched as one white subordinate after another resigned their post. Their excuses were not related to me but the independent school library community is relatively small, so I learned from other colleagues that my staff found me "difficult." And, to make matters worse, my immediate supervisor also blamed me. At one point, he proclaimed that there could be "no more personnel issues in the library or I would face consequences". My boss was unwilling to consider that my staff issues were racial in nature, and not work related. But, because I did not feel supported, I did not feel like I could address his bias, or the bias of my all white staff.

At the time this edict made my job very stressful. I felt like l had no support and that anything I did would result in my losing my job. In the midst of this turmoil, my boss was promoted, and I got a new boss. My new boss was aware of the issues in my department. However, he took a different approach. First, he got to know me. He talked to me and spent time with me. Second, he did not simply believe the words of others about me. He asked me questions that no one else had ever asked me, and when I needed support he provided it. Finally, he gave me positive feedback and told me that it was clear that I was not difficult and that I was not the problem in my department. With my subordinates, my boss also questioned them and listened. However, he did not allow them to make me the scapegoat. He required them to substantiate their claims. When they could not, he refused to let them engage in character assassination. Within weeks, these problems in my department disappeared, and I felt vindicated and respected. When supported adequately, being a good mentor means making good choices that alleviate many of the pitfalls and setbacks that diminish the potential of a librarian of color. People of all color do increasingly better in their jobs when they are positively mentored.

Mentors often come into situations with their biases, and in an attempt not to seem biased, prejudice or bigoted, they make crucial errors in judgment. Statements like "I don't see color" or "you're playing the color card" are attempts to avoid discomfort around race. Mentors not only need to see color, but they need to confront their discomfort with racial issues. Racism is a systemic problem and the fact that our profession is 88% white would lead one to believe that we are a lot more racist than we want to admit. Mentors need, to be honest with themselves and work on cultural competency skills if they find themselves lacking. Being competent monitor is not about being a White Knight or a savior. It's about supporting a work environment that has standards that are applied fairly to every individual, and to do this Librarians of Color need to know what the standard are and how they apply in all situations.

Most importantly, Mentors must not make the mistake of blaming or shaming Librarians of Color when they realize their discomfort around race. Blaming and shaming can take the form of Blaming the victim, proclaiming we are in a post-racial world, or isolating an incident and not acknowledging that it's a example of a systemic problem.

Being a good mentor means making healthy choices. When decisions are made with a clarity of purpose, mentors can help alleviate many of the pitfalls and setbacks that diminish the potential of a Librarian of Color.

Librarians of Color have an obligation to mentor young librarians early and often.

Finally Librarians of Color must mentor others in our profession. We need to make a point of reaching out to graduate student's co-workers and new Librarians. We need to pass on our collective wisdom and be a sounding for new generation of Librarians with generations' old complaints. Further, we need to work with Library programs and University's to develop classes in cultural competencies that are mandatory. We need to work with the American Library Association to adopt cultural competency guidelines for all library workers, and we need to find venues for Librarians to mentor via Facebook, Twitter and other online avenues.

Mentors of color also need to acknowledge that they have to mentor cross-racially as well. Who better to teach you white librarians about the experience of a person of color than their Mentor of color. Librarians of Color have to show our peers and our colleagues how to treat people of color. This tutelage benefits the work place, and it helps our patrons. When we are in positions of authority, we can make a positive impact. While it may seem like it is s someone else's responsibility, it is not. We need to be the change we want to see, and that included Mentoring cross-culturally.

When all else fails find a mentor in another who is not a Librarian

Lastly, studies show that librarians who receive mentoring are ultimately more successful. If you cannot find a mentor within your Library, find out in another area of your life. Mentors come in all shapes and sizes don't be afraid to find someone that can assess your strengths and weakness, and help you when needed. While having a professional mentor is ideal, many of the problems that Librarians of color face, are issues that other people of color face in their professions as well. We can all support each other. R-each out to individuals who are successful in their fields and ask them to mentor you. Resolving many of the above issues can lead to healthier work environments and more retention of library staff.

## Retention

Retention of librarians of color has many challenges. In conversations with other Latinx librarians, Lopez has found that they share the same feelings of isolation and marginalization. In his writing "Leadership in Libraries," San Francisco City Librarian Luis Herrera writes about the results of a survey he conducted with Latinx librarians. He notes the "shared sense of frustration in feeling trapped and typecast to duties related to their ethnicity and not their expertise" (Herrera 130). Other issues that emerged in Herrera's survey were Latinx librarians often feeling added pressure to prove their competence and worth and though no mention of overt racism was made, "the lack of acceptance and cultural insensitivity translated to perceived institutional racism." This cultural disconnect contributes to a disconnect from the larger organizational culture (Herrera 130).

Suggestions for Retention:

• Competitive wages and benefits despite the fact that the library profession is predominantly female, a wage gap still exists: In 2014, women working as full-time librarians reported a median annual salary of $48,589, compared to $52,528 for men. Among librarians with a Master's degree working 32 hours a week or more in colleges, universities, and professional schools, including junior colleges, women earned 90% of what men earned in 2014. Black librarians in higher education working full-time earned just 90% of what their White counterparts earned (Library Workers, 2017).

• Mentorship, including helping librarians of color navigate their way through moving up the ladder into leadership roles

• Welcoming programs--connecting with other staff increases retention

• Professional development (and release time for it)

• Orientations that include clear expectations and training on the culture of the workplace as well information on any affinity groups

• Supportive supervisor relationships

• Cultural competency training during onboarding for all staff, including training on having those difficult conversations that challenge white fragility

• I ncrease sensitivity toward other cultures/groups helps retention, builds empathy through cross-cultural learning, and provides the support and opportunities for minority librarians to grow into leadership positions on par with their white colleagues. Academic libraries can make use of this to help underrepresented students gain the experience needed be as successful as their white counterparts and build the inclusive environment that will carry over to public libraries (Pho 2014).

• Create a culture of inclusion that provides mentors and builds long-term employment, and make it explicit in hiring that diverse backgrounds are valued. This fosters honest relationships and helps all employees feel supported, that they belong, and that they are free to express themselves (Pho 2014).

• Mindfulness that diversity goes beyond race and ethnicity.

This list is not meant to be all inclusive, but the suggestions are mindful ways to help broach the subject and provide some ideas for administrators and managers to improve work environments for librarians of color. While all of this points to the very real struggle librarians of color face in a predominately white field, we must also keep in mind that the work itself can be very rewarding. We have seen the impact that our work has had on our patrons—particularly in the youth that we serve.

Lastly, to combat feelings of isolation (especially if you are a solitary person of color in your library) I would also suggest connecting with your colleagues through groups like REFORMA and the Black Caucus of the American Library Association. Find out if there is a local chapter. Last year with the support of her Library Director, Diana Lopez co-coordinated a meeting of Bibliotecas Para la Gente, a Bay Area local chapter of REFORMA. We had a great turnout, and Luis Herrera, San Francisco City Librarian, attended and spoke at the meeting. The event reenergized the group, and colleagues from the North Bay were happy to be able to attend a meeting that was closer to them. Diana recently ran into Luis at the California Library Association Conference, and he shared a story with her about a colleague who had attended and found the meeting so inspirational that she implemented a new program at her system. And always remember the impact that you have on the youth in your library. You are a role model for them and a representation of a profession that they too can someday join and in turn reach other youth. You can be that librarian that looks like them and with whom they feel a distinct connection with.

# Critlib Management: Leading and Inspiring Through a Social Justice Framework

Candise Branum
Oregon College of Oriental Medicine

## Critlib Management: Leading and Inspiring Through a Social Justice Framework

Critlib, or critical librarianship, is the discussion and application of social justice in the library field. Generally, the application of critlib has been focused on information literacy and pedagogy and cataloging, but one important aspect of the discussion that is often overlooked is that of library management. Just like teaching, many librarians are not trained specifically to be library managers -- being a good manager is something we learn on the job, lived experience, and professional development. Critlib is based in both theory and practice, and we must make a conscious effort to teach ourselves about the ways in which social justice can be applied to library practices. Critlib praxis is something we continuously work on, both within ourselves and within our communities and libraries; library management is just one aspect of our work that can be reevaluated through a feminist lens.

Management, in general, is not glamourous. Critical pedagogy and radical cataloging are exciting to talk about because we choose to be instructional librarians and catalogers, but management is something many of us simply fall into. While there are definitely librarians who strive for high-level administrative positions, many of us came into this profession passionate about social justice issues, and did not expect to find ourselves in leadership positions. Management has been something learned on the job, over multiple careers, but never something I explicitly sought out or critically evaluated until recently. I've always viewed middle management as being a tool of the establishment, towing the line but not pushing too many boundaries. Even while being a library director myself, the images that came to mind when I thought about management in general were stereotypical: White. Male. Patriarchal. Conservative.

These ideas about management stemmed mostly from the media and not my own personal experience with management. I grew up working class, and my parents, extended family, and neighbors were solidly blue collar. While blue collar work had a history of union organizing and solidarity work, white collar work seemed apolitical and individualistic. In actuality, management is all about human interaction. With some level of control over the operations of an organization, managers have the power to either maintain the status quo or to break down barriers that prevent inclusive and collaborative work. Thinking about management in this light has been extremely powerful for me; it allows me to reframe my contributions as integral to forwarding social justice work in librarianship. Also, it is absolutely vital to systemic change to be able to make changes within an organization, and create systems of support that redirect power imbalances. Library managers are fundamental to this work.

In this essay, I will discuss the power of acknowledging trauma and the ways library managers can explicitly address national issues of inequity. I will discuss the importance of librarians in advocating for social justice through basic diversity and inclusion projects, as well as through in-depth systemic changes. Finally, I will touch on campus activism, illustrating some of the ways that academic libraries can engage in social justice work by advocating for campus-wide policy changes, social justice-oriented trainings, and participating in national activist solidarity movements, such as Libraries 4 Black Lives.

## Orlando

On June 13th, 2016, I showed up for work and people on campus acted like it was just a normal Monday. For many people, it probably was. Mass shootings are frighteningly normal now, and though queer people have come to know and expect a level of violence (both from our history and our lived experiences), the massacre at the Pulse Nightclub in Orlando felt anything but normal. Those in the queer community felt as if we had lost something enormous. Fifty magical lives were extinguished, and with them, any vestige of our sense of safety. In the aftermath, many of us isolated ourselves because we didn't want to have to explain to our straight friends and colleagues that one of the reasons we were feeling so shocked from this particular incident was that it was a wake-up call.

Even in the most progressive of cities, you still have to take stock of where you are at and who is around you before giving your partner a kiss or holding their hand. We've learned to do this unconsciously, but we still do it. Physical safety is still the biggest issue for the queer community; the number of trans women, and specifically trans women of color, who are murdered each year is actually increasing (Human Rights Campaign, 2016). On the morning of June 13th, 2016, I tried to put on a smile and go about my regular work day. Then, one of my student workers, who is a gay man, came in. I asked him how he was holding up. "Not good," he responded, as tears started to wedge through his barely held-together facade. I hugged him tightly, tighter than I've ever hugged an employee or student, and we cried in each other's arms at the library circulation desk. We didn't have to talk about what had happened or why it hurt, because we both knew it and felt it, both in our own lives and shared histories.

I was in mourning, and it seemed like the straight people in my life didn't understand that this was something that needed to be acknowledged. The college administration was noticeably silent on the issue, and I felt it. The lack of public statement, especially knowing that so many of our students identify as members of the LGBTQ community, was isolating. It created a gulf between those who felt the trauma in their bones, and those who saw this as just another shooting. I didn't really know what, if anything, the college administration could do, but as one of my friends noted on Facebook, "The silence from straight people [was] deafening."

So, I spoke up as an administrator; inside my institution, I have voice and power. I emailed the College President and our Director of Communications and Outreach, and plainly stated that the silence from the college administration was unacceptable. They were completely sympathetic, and moved quickly to rectify the situation by making a public statement and creating a space on campus where we could express our heartache. In addition, a grief counselor was invited to campus, and a wall in the main entrance was dedicated to allowing community members to post messages of love and anguish.

I think about my experience as a queer woman and the sorrow and trauma I felt over Orlando, and I can't help but think about how racially motivated violence affects the African American community, both historically and currently, and how numb society seems to be over the violence perpetuated on black bodies. Lackluster excuses have been made justifying the assault on people of color since the birth of this nation, and though the current cluster of police shootings of unarmed Black Americans is nothing new, it does not mean that we should not be outraged. Just because we recognize that we live in a nation governed by White Supremacy doesn't mean we shouldn't be heartbroken and outraged when we witness evidence of hatred and bigotry.

When college administrators say nothing about these shootings, it sends the message that they are normal. One administrator at OCOM, while acknowledging the need for the college to address the violence being perpetrated against people of color, wondered aloud how we could work to address the murders of African Americans by the police force when it happens so frequently. Do we send out a separate formal message for every new life destroyed? How do we show support in a powerful and ongoing way without our message becoming diluted? This is actually an important question -- it demonstrates both the numbing repetition of violence we are dealing with, along with the overwhelming feelings of not knowing how to best use one's power and privilege to elicit change.

## Making Statements and Setting the Tone

One thing I realized from my experience following the Orlando shootings was this: simply acknowledging the trauma that people may be feeling might seem like a small gesture, but it is an important step in supporting your staff and community members. Staff shouldn't have to ask for support, and by proactively addressing issues that affect our staff and community members, we are sending the message that we are allies. When Terence Crutcher became the fourth unarmed black man to be killed in the month of September, 2016, I brought it up to administrators at our college that we had yet to acknowledge the effect that police shootings of unarmed Black Americans had on our community.

After writing a passionate and carefully worded email to the President of our college, waiting to hear her response made me extremely nervous; I knew administrators at my institution felt strongly about social justice, but how far would this extend? Although there was nothing in the college's history to suggest this, I was scared that they wouldn't have my back, and that they would not want to start a scary and messy discussion of racial politics on campus. As it turned out, I had nothing to fear; upper-level administration noted that social justice was a part of the college's values statement, and they agreed that it was important to address this and future social justice issues publicly.

While looking to see how other academic institutions were addressing racial violence in the United States, I found a few excellent examples of public statements put out by high-level administrators, including statements from the Chancellor of UNC and the President of MIT. The most successful of these statements blended not only compassion and a promise of support for the community, but also included plans for action, including programming that allows for campus-wide conversations about inclusion, diversity, and racial violence. MIT's President Reif (2016) spoke of the fear and helplessness that many feel, but advocated for the institution's community members to use their skills to work towards positive change:

> *Injustice, racism, mistrust, suspicion, fear and violence corrode the foundations of a healthy society. We cannot stand as observers and accept a future of escalating violence and divisiveness. I believe our leading civic institutions have a responsibility to speak clearly against these corrosive forces and to act practically to inspire and create positive change. In this time of need, the MIT community has an opportunity to offer service of great value to our society, to our country and perhaps to the world by applying our unique strengths to the problem at hand* (Reif, 2016, para. 5).

As library managers, we must be explicit and direct in demonstrating our fight against racism, sexism and homophobia. We do this by using our voices. We state specifically, emphatically, that we will not tolerate hate speech of any kind. We vocalize that we are working to ensure that our libraries are truly safe spaces, and that we are allies in the fight to end White Supremacy. Speaking out and using our voices is important to setting the tone of our libraries, and in fostering communities that work to end oppressions. Kim Bohyun (2016) wrote, "Sometimes, saying isn't much. But right now, saying it aloud can mean everything. If you support those who belong to minority groups but don't say it out loud, how would they know it?" (para. 8).

By default, administrators carry some amount of power, and the ability to use our voices in a public way is a privilege. The fears I had around making waves at our institution were complicated. I grew up white, queer, and working class in rural Oregon; education was a saving grace for me, but I've also had to work hard to feel like I belong in academia. Using my position as a leader to speak out about oppression, and making sure changes supporting social justice were enacted at our institution have been particularly empowering acts, especially because I am the first person in my family to graduate from college. But, I also know that my experience is very different from the experiences of academic librarians of color. When our colleagues of color speak up, are they met with support, or with resistance? When our colleagues of color speak up, are they met with defensiveness from White librarians, who feel like any kind of criticism means we aren't being good enough colleagues? Tone policing is very real; those in places of privilege often don't know how to react to the pain, fear and anger expressed by marginalized people, and instead of acknowledging that those feelings are hard and asking how they can help, people often become defensive and attempt to minimize emotions. Regardless of whether emotions are "valid" or not, by creating a safe space for staff to vocalize their concerns, and by truly hearing both the emotions and the "facts," we can work on making changes to create a supportive environment for our staff.

As library managers, we must work to ensure that risks are not just taken on by those with the most to lose, those whose feelings are most often dismissed. As Jessica Anne Bratt, one of the Library Journal 2016 Movers & Shakers noted, "It can be daunting and you sometimes feel, 'if I take a stand, who will defend me?'" (Peet, 2016). White librarians must ensure that systems are in place that give space and power for the voices of librarians of color to be heard. Straight and gender-conforming librarians must speak up about injustices towards the LGBTQ community, so their queer librarian friends don't have to "out" themselves. Being good allies requires us to make sure diverse voices are present, but also step up and not expect minority voices to do all the work.

## Digging Deeper than Diversity Initiatives

Attempts to promote diversity in the academic library setting come from a good place, but often serve to centralize the white experience as normal and true. The very concept of "diversity" is troubling as it focuses on editing, not dismantling, the white dominant paradigm; ensuring diversity of voices is immensely important, but framing those voices in relation to a white, educated, middle-class voice is inherently problematic. In particular, the concept of diversity focuses attention on "othered" groups, and allows dominant groups to simply exist without attracting attention. Hussey (2010, p. 7) notes that, "When past issues of racial discrimination and ethnic oppression are minimized to underrepresentation of certain groups and the inclusion of librarians of color, the roles of white culture and white privilege are not addressed." Discussions about diversity can feel hollow because they frequently are – we often use safe language to dance around the difficult and messy truth of race relations in the United States.

When we think about how libraries in particular promote diversity, the strategies used are often simple and effective, such as creating displays that promote <fill in the blank> Pride Month. If acknowledging trauma is the first step in demonstrating commitment to allied social justice work, developing and supporting programming, and collections that back up these words are the crucial next steps for library management. There are fast, easy, and non-threatening projects that incorporate what we are already doing in libraries: displays, resource guides and focused programming. These projects are not only important for education and visibility, but they also work as a reminder that libraries are safe spaces. They can also be simplistic, and generally are not credited with creating long-lasting change.

However, the that individuals from a marginalized group may feel from seeing themselves represented in programming and collection development is powerful and supports the inclusion of diverse voices. What I am suggesting is for library leaders to continue promoting these kinds of small-scale projects that advance the ideas of diversity and inclusion, but also investigate how these ideas can be embedded into the very structure of our library work. Mathuews (2016) proposes "intentionally incorporating social justice frameworks into common library functions such as information literacy education, research services, access to scholarly material, and physical spaces for scholarly activity and engagement" (p. 6), which would allow continuous, ongoing work towards racial justice and equity. Rather than having an initiative or project with a beginning and end date, actually embedding social justice frameworks into our everyday work is vital to creating lasting change.

## Aligning Values with Language

Academic librarians often see ourselves as radical, but when it comes to pushing the boundaries of our profession, we tend to play it safe. We often think of our roles and our mission as pertaining to the learning needs of our community, but we narrowly define this as how it directly relates to the curriculum, rather than looking at our student body in a holistic way. Even though we may feel strongly about an issue, we were told in library school to be impartial, and approach all queries with a neutral stance. On this point, I vehemently disagree. Neutrality is by default a political statement; it indicates that you have the privilege to stay silent, that your body and mental health and safety are not at stake. Rabbi Prinz once noted that, "Bigotry and hatred are not the most urgent problems. The most urgent, the most disgraceful, the most shameful and most tragic problem is silence" (Cone, 2004, p. 150). The act of neutrality is the act of siding with the status quo and refusing to be an ally. For librarians of conscience, neutrality is not an option.

Even worse, some dispassionate librarians may argue that if the issue doesn't seem to directly affect our students or our mission statement, then it is not our place to address it. I would argue that all social justice issues affect our communities. Just because our campus hasn't reported any sexual assaults in the past year doesn't mean our students don't think about it, or that they haven't been personally affected by sexual violence. A recent editorial by Monnica Williams (2016) published on PBS spoke to the trauma inflicted upon people of color by continually witnessing racial violence, and how videos showing police shootings of Black Americans reinforces the trauma of racism. The traumatic effects of witnessing violence that targets individuals based on sexual preference, race, religion or gender affects not just members of those groups, but our entire society. While we can't purport to make assumptions about what specific issues will trigger our students, what we do know is that students have come to expect discussions about social justice issues. "In a study of the classroom climate in higher education, Boysen (2012) found that students expect faculty to confront social justice issues in the classroom" (Mathuews, 2016, p. 9).

Social justice and inequality affect our learning communities; our mission statements should address this, and if they don't, library managers must advocate for changes. Kim Moreland of the Portland Development Commission suggested that organizations explicitly state that they are anti-racist in their mission statements (Moreland, Nguyen, & Sadruddin, 2016). Incorporating clear anti-racist language into mission statements and other documentation will hold organizations accountable, and make sure that diversity initiatives are not viewed as side-projects, but as an integral part of the organization. Integrating social justice work as a part of an organization's mission allows it to prevent diversity and inclusion initiatives from being the first on the chopping block when budget cuts arise.

Library directors who have the power to make changes at a departmental level can use this opportunity to work with their staff in creating mission statements that are inclusive and reflective of the organization's social justice goals, but the next step should be advocating for adopting an explicitly anti-racist position in the larger institutional mission statement. "Education's role is to challenge inequality and dominant myths rather than socialize students in the status quo. Learning is directed toward social change and transforming the world, and 'true' learning empowers students to challenge oppression in their lives" (Stage, Muller, Kinzie, & Simmons, 1998, p. 57); if this is true, then the framework for our work must be documented with anti-racist, inclusive language.

## Implementing Social Justice Library Work

In a recent "Conversation About Diversity" held at OCOM, staff was encouraged to take some of the ideas discussed at the panel presentation and run with them. We had a great, open conversation about practical ways that the college could make changes, but the lingering question that was vocalized over and over throughout the wrap-up was, "What's my part? What comes next?" College administration can say that they support diversity initiatives, but if structures are not in place to facilitate the transformation of those ideas into actionable items, then staff may not prioritize social justice work over the everyday work that they are expected to do.

I like to think that we all come from good places; we want to think the best of one another, but as Waleed Sadruddin (Moreland, Nguyen, & Sadruddin, 2016) noted, you can't expect niceness to fix the issue. We must understand that the act of caring doesn't actually solve issues as complex as discrimination and lack of inclusiveness, and that we must use metrics and actually push the envelope to create change. In order to create institutional changes that actually last, library leaders must facilitate the creation of organizational programs that ensure that diversity, inclusion and social justice goals are met. Library managers have to make sure social justice and diversity workshops and trainings are built into professional development budgets, and that our staff have the opportunity to work on not only their technical skills but on being a better, more compassionate workforce.

We often think of this type of work as a sidebar to the regular work that we do, but it is completely connected to the way we interact with one another, and even the services we provide. As managers, it is our responsibility to ensure our staff obtain training that goes beyond basic introductions, and incorporates concepts of tolerance and diversity. Smaller libraries could even partner with other libraries outside of their institution, which would allow them to share expenses, and broaden the expanse of their professional development offerings.

In addition to staff training and development, it is important to create a system that holds library management accountable. Having a system in place that has institutional buy-in will allow us to track the work library management does to ensure that our diversity and inclusion goals are being met. One method that library leaders can adopt to aid in this process is Multicultural Organizational Development (MCOD). MCOD is a six-stage process of best practices that aids organizations in progressing towards "socially just, inclusive campus communities" (Wall & Obear, 2008, p. 1) in an intentional and proactive way. One aspect that MCOD speaks to is that "systems, not just individuals, must be the focus of change" (Obear & Kerr, 2015, p. 138); this is exactly the kind of work a library manager can accomplish – systems-level work to help create a truly inclusive community.

In addition to utilizing this process in our libraries, we should also be pushing administration to adopt an institution-wide MCOD process. It is great if the library is doing its part, but we have to look at college campuses in a holistic way as well: if one part is resistant or hostile, this will have a negative effect on all of the other departments. The Association of Research Libraries (ARL) SPEC Kit 319 (Maxey-Harris & Anaya, 2010) is another great tool that specifically addresses academic library diversity plans and programs. This toolkit includes examples of diversity plans from academic libraries to aid those who are interested in developing programs of their own. This is maybe the most important work that we can do as library managers: a supportive framework ensure that social justice work is integrated into our everyday work, thus normalizing it.

## Taking Action

Libraries 4 Black Lives is a Movement for Black Lives affinity group comprised of library workers, activists, and archivists committed to racial equity. This recently formed group is calling on librarians across the country to publicly show support and join the cause: "We publicly affirm our support for the Movement for Black Lives and we commit to deepening racial equity work in our institutions and communities" (Libraries 4 Black Lives, 2016b, para. 5) In addition to confirming the importance of the work that libraries already do in striving towards inclusion, the group is interested in investigating how libraries can "address systemic racial injustice and implicit personal bias" (Libraries 4 Black Lives, 2016a, para. 4). I am extremely excited for L4BL's potential, alongside other progressive librarian groups, to begin the formalized process of supporting each other in our work concerning social equity.

The rise in reported violence against communities of color and LGBTQ folk is directly related to the recent election of Donald Trump as the President of the United States and the need for librarians to commit to working towards social justice has only increased. Library staff can work towards these goals, but management must ensure that frameworks are in place to support staff in this work. In discussing how the public library in Ferguson, MO opted to stay open during city-wide protests in order to support the needs of the community, Carla Hayden stated that library administrators must act as the "anchor" in times of crisis: "It's critical to have your administrators ready to go to the sites to be the backup for the regular staff. You may not be fighting, but you're in the fight" (Cottrell, 2015). We are all in the fight.

The bullying tactics of White Supremacists have been reported at college campuses across the United States (Dickerson & Saul, 2016), making students who are Black, Muslim, Jewish, queer, and/or female-identified fearful for their physical safety. Racism and sexism have always been pervasive issues on college campuses, but the change in presidency has invoked a rising culture of intimidation and fear that permeates our communities, even in the supposedly progressive academic environment. It is not possible to create inclusive, positive learning environments when students fear for their physical safety. This is what we have to contend with. This is what is at stake.

As library administrators, we have power to make changes to create and promote diverse collections and communities to vocalize the library's role as a safe space, and to create organizational frameworks that support our staff in social justice work. Being a library manager means using our voices and our power to be leaders in the fight, and to provide supportive platforms. It means providing leadership during stressful periods, but also being able to take a step back and allow other voices to take center stage.

Figure 6

# Prison Libraries: On the Fringe of the Library World

Mary Rayme
Huttonsville Correctional Center
Huttonsville, West Virginia

## Abstract

The United States has the largest incarcerated population in the world with an estimate of 2.3 million held in prisons and jails nationwide as of 2016. However, in the professional librarian field, prison libraries and librarians are largely underrepresented and considered as a library job of last resort. The lack of representation of prison librarians and of prison library jobs may be based on the negative perception of criminals and the incarcerated. According to statistics, 95% of incarcerated people eventually return to the general public. The goal of prison libraries is to educate, empower, and entertain inmates so that they may be peaceful prisoners as well as contributing members of society once they reintegrate into the outside world. There are few online or professional groups for prison library support and there are no library degrees offered that specialize in serving prison libraries. While library conferences may offer sessions for public and school librarians, there are few, if any, educational offerings for librarians who work in jails and prisons.

There are also few grant or funding opportunities for prison libraries. In contrast to the perception of prison libraries, these institutions may have some of the highest circulation rates per capita of any public, school, or academic library. While prison librarians may be largely ignored in the professional library field, the career rewards make up for any lack of professional support. While anecdotally many inmates report that they rarely or never visited a library "on the outside", many have the opportunity to become avid and lifelong learners while serving a sentence in a correctional facility. Isolated inmates are grateful for books and services provided in a prison library. The prison library provides a peaceful and stimulating oasis in a stressful and regulated environment. It is rewarding, and oftentimes joyous, not only to recommend a book but to assist another human being return to society as responsible citizens.

**Prison Libraries: On the Fringe of the Library World**

Prison libraries are unique, important, and largely underrepresented in the field.

In the professional library world in the United States, prison libraries are Special Libraries, classified and included with art libraries, academic libraries, business/law libraries, medical libraries, and the like. The public librarian and the school librarian perhaps represent the largest percentage of professional librarians. The American Library Association has a promotional that says, "There are more public libraries than McDonald's™ in the U.S.—a total of 16,766 including branches" (American Library Association, 2015).

In contrast, a report from the Washington Post states there are more prisons and jails than degree-granting colleges and universities in the United States (Washington Post, 2016). At slightly over 5,000 prisons and jails in the United States, the number of professional librarians serving these institutions is woefully low and difficult to calculate. The American Library Association has a Prison Librarian list-serv with less than 100 subscribing. Inclusion of prison libraries as a topic has been very sparse at annual conferences of the American Library Association--another indicator of lack of engagement and unity of professional prison librarians. While the ALA has published a powerful statement entitled Prisoners' Right to Read, it is merely an expression and not a legally binding document. (American Library Association, 2014).

A chart from the American Library Association breaks down the number of paid librarians in the United States as:

Public Libraries, 136,851

Public School Libraries, 126,010

Private School Libraries, 17,860

Academic Libraries, 85,751 (American Library Association, 2015)

At a time when the United States has the largest imprisoned population in the world--

2.2 million--professional prison librarians are a rare and minority population (United States Department of Justice, 2016). This researcher speculates that with the large number of imprisoned people, the need has never been greater for professional librarians who serve the incarcerated, and yet research, articles, professional support, and literature are lacking in guiding this field. There are no professional Prison Librarian groups or organizations in the United States that are exclusive to this field.

In graduate school at the University of Tennessee, aspiring librarians pursued coursework in collection development, classification and cataloging, young adult services, children's literature, and public librarianship. This program focused on educating academic, public, special, and school librarians and yet this American Library Association-approved program offered no courses or coursework in prison librarianship.

## Library Services and Technology Act

The Institute for Museum and Library Services is a federal entity providing funding for State Library Administrative Agencies (SLAA) that is federally mandated via the Library Services and Technology Act (LSTA). From the IMLS website, "The Grants to States program allocates a base amount to each of the SLAAs plus a supplemental amount based on population. For each of the 50 states, Puerto Rico and the District of Columbia, the base amount is $680,000 each, and for the U.S. Territories the base amount is $60,000 each." According to a senior program officer at the IMLS, the base amount of $680,000 is in accordance with legislation. It is of interest to note that this base amount doubled in 2010 from $340,000 (email, November 10, 2016). If a state such as West Virginia is losing population, the state loses funding from the LSTA. In West Virginia, prison libraries were supported by funding from the state's library commission until the late 20th century. As population in West Virginia has dwindled, so has its funding and functions.

A survey of all state library entities conducted by this researcher revealed that very few states offer direct monetary support to jails and prisons (See appendix A). Many state library representatives mentioned that they provide support via inter-library loan or, that grant funding was available through LSTA, but the overall message is that in the professional library world prison libraries are not a priority.

## Some States Support Prison Libraries

Despite the lack of a unified front, there are some places in the United States where prisons and detention centers are thriving with the help of state library commissions, public libraries, and librarians. The New York Public Library is an excellent example of a state library entity that has partnered with prisons and jails to create programs and resources for the incarcerated. Connections is an annual publication of New York Public Libraries that is aimed to assist the imprisoned with reentry to the outside world. This complete bilingual resource guide of 150 pages contains information regarding education, housing, financial assistance, mental health, and legal services. Connections was created in 1982 by Steve Likosky, New York's first correctional services librarian (Connections, 2016). This same publication estimates 7 million adults in the United States are incarcerated or under correctional control such as parole or probation. In other words, "About 1 in 36 adults (or 2.8% of adults in the United States) was under some form of correctional supervision at yearend 2014..." (United States Department of Justice, 2016).

States such as Oklahoma and Wyoming provide modest funds for state prisons to purchase books (email, November 6, 2016). The state library entities currently providing exemplary service for prison libraries include Colorado, Washington, and New York. For example, the Colorado State Library cooperates with the Colorado Department of Corrections, Colorado Human Services, and the Colorado Department of Education to "hire and manage library staff, fund general operating expenses, designate space for their libraries, and provide limited funds for books and equipment" (Brochure, Colorado State Library 2016). Colorado also provides library services for mental health facilities, state veterans' homes, and the Colorado School for the Deaf and Blind (Colorado Institutional Library Development, 2016). To quote from the Colorado Department of Education's website, "The Colorado State Library's Institutional Library Development unit and the staff of the Colorado Correctional Libraries believe that libraries have the power to change the world 'one reader at a time.' Many of us find prisoners to be the most appreciative and enthusiastic library users we've ever worked with, and serving them to be the most gratifying work we've ever done" (Prison Libraries, 2016).

## Why the Lack of Prison Librarians?

So why are there so few professional prison librarians in the United States? This researcher speculates that the status of criminals plays a large part in this inequity. In many ways, citizens on the outside of prison have knowledge of criminals through television and the genre of true crime books. Contemporary television shows such as Law and Order, CSI, Bones, and The Closer show criminals as evil wrong-doers who deserve to be imprisoned without luxuries for their actions. Many times in popular culture, criminals are the black and white, black hat- wearing bad guys who have gotten what they deserve. Only more recent popular cultural offerings such as Orange is the New Black and Blacklist show the criminal as a nuanced human being capable of both good and evil. In our contemporary national psyche, criminals are perceived as bad people nor do they deserve the service of professional librarians. This researcher speculates that the low status of criminals and inmates may transfer in some way to the professionals who serve them.

Another challenge to the world of professional prison librarians is that each state has different policies for prison libraries. In the United States, inmates are required by law to have access to an up-to-date and effective law library seven days a week (Lewis v. Casey, 1996). However, there is no stipulation in the law regarding the breadth and quality of that law library. There is also no law that mandates that prisoners must have a recreational lending library. While the New York Public Library has the librarians and funds to publish reentry outreach materials for inmates, West Virginia and many other states do not enjoy such resources. In short, states with more money have the opportunity to provide better funded libraries and services for prisoners. In 2015, the Oklahoma Department of Libraries spent $45,858 to purchase books for 15 correctional centers (email, November 6, 2016). While this averages out to be a little over $3,000 per facility, even this is more than most state library entities provide.

What many on the outside of a prison may not understand is that most criminals continue to pay for their crimes well after their prison sentences are completed. Convicted felons have a difficult time finding employment and a place to live upon release. Sex offenders, in particular, continue to be demonized after they serve a sentence by being registered as such. In the U.S., the time a sex offender spends on that register varies by state and by the sentence of an individual. While West Virginia mandates that sex offenders be registered for five years, a judge may order a lifetime registrant in the case of a particularly heinous crime. The fact that sex offenders are placed on a registry is a reflection of how much we value children as a country. This same value placed on children is perhaps a reason why, alternatively, public school and public librarians are at the top of the librarian status heap.

This researcher found only a handful of grant opportunities available for prison libraries. In contrast, there are many grants available for school and public libraries. Several of the state library entities contacted by this researcher mention that grant funding is available through LSTA; these states include Florida, Utah, and California. Some also mention that they have not received grant requests from state correctional facilities recently. In October 2012, the California State Library (CSL) provided a sizeable grant to the Southern California Library Cooperative (SCLC) for "$371,000 to provide textbooks and recreational reading materials to California Prisons (CSL, 2012)".

### The Second Chance Act – Pell Grant Revived

Education is an important part of reducing recidivism. Studies have shown that inmates who receive vocational training or achieve their GED while incarcerated are significantly less likely to reoffend. To quote from a 2013 article from the Rand Corporation, "Researchers found that inmates who participate in correctional education programs have 43% lower odds of returning to prison than those who do not." The role of the prison library, and therefore the prison librarian, is vital not just to inmates but to law-abiding citizens who may one day work or live with former felons. One might even view education as crime prevention.

Perhaps in response to the high rate of U.S. incarceration, President Barrack Obama lifted the ban on Pell Grants to felons and has registered approximately 12,000 prisoners to receive education in a pilot program. This experimental and collaborative program provides meaningful education and experience to inmates who may pursue degrees such as an Associate of Science in Business or Land Surveying Technology, a Bachelor of Science in Business Administration, or a Bachelor of Arts in Natural Resource Management (Glenville State College, 2016). While a press release from the U.S. Department of Education says, "to test whether participation in high quality education programs increases after expanding access to financial aid for incarcerated individuals," this researcher speculates that the inmate college students will be tracked in the years to come to reinforce the idea that education reduces recidivism (USDE, 2016). Additionally, a Rand Corporation study revealed that "a $1 investment in prison education reducing incarceration costs by $4 to $5 during the first three years post-release" (Rand Corporation, 2013). Educating inmates is an excellent financial and social investment.

## Jail vs. Prison

Many people unfamiliar with the correctional system in the United States may use the words "jail" and "prison" interchangeably but these two entities are quite different. In general terms, jails are for people with sentences of a year or less. Prisons are for housing inmates with felony charges serving longer sentences. In jails, there may not be a law library or a reading library with professional librarians available to answer reference questions or provide interlibrary loaned books. At a local regional jail in West Virginia, the library is a cart of books that is wheeled around regularly for inmates to make a limited reading selection. In defense of the lack of in-depth legal resources at most jails, the shorter length of sentences of most jailed inmates makes many legal actions (which may take years) to be impractical.

## Fear of Violence and Personal Safety

Perhaps another contributing factor to the lack of prison librarians is fear of violence and safety working in a corrections environment. Medium to maximum security prisons may be especially dangerous places where murderers, rapists, and sex offenders all do time. This researcher suggests that librarians and library patrons (especially in metropolitan areas) may be just as susceptible to violence and injury. A quick Google News search of the words "library" and "assault" show recent incidents of violence at Portland State University in Portland, Oregon, the Aldine Branch Library in Houston, Texas, the University of New Mexico in Albuquerque, New Mexico, and the North Branch Public Library in Memphis, Tennessee. All of these assaults occurred in libraries in November 2016. Public libraries may be especially dangerous because they are open to anyone. When this researcher searched "prison library" and "assault" there was one news story from 2008: a prison librarian at Maine State Prison was tied to her desk and tortured for hours (Steeves, 2010). While prison may be a dangerous place there are measures in place–correctional officers, policies, cameras, and radios--that ensure order and safety.

## Which Librarians Get Paid the Most?

Some might think that prison librarians are paid less than other professional librarians yet this researcher found that this is not the case. According to a Library Journal article, school librarians had the highest median salary at $58,000, academic librarians had a mean salary of $53,000, and special librarians had a mean aggregate salary of $52,334 (Library Journal, 2014). To quote from a more recent article, "School libraries, special libraries, and other kinds of organizations ($48,588, $48,536, and $48,424, respectively) reported salaries slightly above the overall average (+3.1%)." (Library Journal, 2015) Prison librarians seem to be paid about as much as other professional librarians.

## Prison Libraries Can Be Hyperactive

Circulation statistics are often used by professional librarians as an indicator of the health of their library. While prison librarians may be low in status in the professional field, prison libraries may have some of the highest circulation numbers per capita of any public or academic library. In the prison where this researcher works, there are 1,135 inmates and the library holds about 10,000 books. In 2015, the library accumulated approximately 75,000 circulations--the equivalent of all inmates reading about 66 books per year.

## Conclusions

While prison libraries continue to be largely ignored in the professional library world, there is not much that separates this profession from any other form of librarianship. Collection development, reference services, cataloging, and tracking statistics are all part of a prison librarian's job. Programming, technology, reader's advisory, and inter-library loans are also part of prison librarianship. This researcher speculates that the demonized criminal affects the status level of working as a prison librarian. To put it simply—because criminals are not important, neither are prison librarians.

For librarians who desire to work with underserved populations, criminals are one of the most universally disliked populations and therefore one of the neediest. Because of the large population of incarcerated individuals in the United States, the need for energized and educated prison librarians has never been greater. Since research shows the important connection between education and recidivism, this is another vital opportunity for librarians who want to make a positive change in the world. This researcher suggests that prison librarians who educate, empower, and entertain inmates through libraries are an important part of crime prevention. Reading promotes imagination, which in turn promotes empathy. Before one can have empathy, one must be able to imagine themselves in another's place. Empathy promotes prosocial behavior, one of the building blocks of criminal reformation.

In a quote that is often attributed to Sanford Bates, the first director of the Federal Bureau of Prisons, "Individuals are sent to prison as punishment, not for punishment." If the purpose of incarceration is to reform and rehabilitate, the importance of prison libraries--and therefore prison librarians--cannot be overstated. The challenging and rewarding work environment of the prison librarian deserves to be taught in universities in ALA-accredited library programs. Prison librarians deserve at least one professional organization who champions their unique positions and offers conferences that address the contemporary corrections issues. As degreed professionals who work behind bars and razor wire every day, prison librarians need a unified front that expresses the true importance of this under-represented niche of librarianship.

# The Remix: Hip Hop Information Literacy Pedagogy in the 21st Century

kYmberly Keeton, M.L.S.

*"I love who you are, I love who you ain't."* - Andre 3000
## Mic_Check 1.2.3. I Now in Session

Hip Hop Information Literacy is comprised of a group of knowledge practices that are necessary for students in an academic setting to be cognizant of how to find, retrieve, evaluate, apply, and acknowledge cultural, visual, and data literacy information in the digital age. The methodology is based on the Association of College & Research Libraries (ACRL) Framework for Information Literacy for Higher Education and uses its core concepts for literacy and research, implemented with flexible options to practice within any discipline in academia. Students should be able to determine the extent of information, access needed information, evaluate information, and use information effectively and legally. Equally important is the environment in which they learn. Ken Blain (2004) author of the book, What the Best College Teachers Do, suggests:

> ...*The best teachers often try to create what we have come to call a "natural critical learning environment." In that environment, people learn by confronting intriguing, beautiful, or important problem, authentic tasks that will challenge them to grapple with ideas, rethink their assumptions, and examine their mental modes of reality* (p. 18).

Using Hip Hop as the thematic content to teach these skills allows students in a collaborative environment to be culturally connected to classroom instruction. Since Hip Hop emerged as a cultural and political movement in the early 1970s, it has become a creative-Mecca for underground artists, rappers, dancers, and DJ's in American culture; as a movement, Hip Hop has created creative citizens that have turned into a force to be reckoned with over the last four decades. Introducing students to the history of the art form, and exposing them to research skills that allow them the opportunity to form a thesis about the movement will facilitate critical thinking skills and engender resilient research practices that convey this consensus. Through Hip Hop education, I personally have the opportunity to discuss social, political and cultural themes with students that awakens their senses and gives permission to proceed to research, collaborate, write, and think critically.

*"If knowledge is the key then just show me the lock."* - ATQC

## Introduction

Marcella Runell (2006), a Hip Hop educator states in the article Hip Hop Education 101, "Public schools in urban areas are like what hip hop once was: under-resourced, ripe for social change, and full of organic creativity," (Runnell, 2006, p. 1). In like manner, academic universities can be observed in the same scope in the 21st century. The question has always been how to meet students where they are; using Hip Hop as thematic content provides the opportunity to simultaneously discuss social and cultural issues from the past and present. As a new Academic Librarian and Assistant Professor of Library Science at an (HBCU) Historically Black College University, designing Hip Hop Information Literacy emerged from teaching one semester of general Information Literacy. Students seemed bored and disillusioned with the content and the environment. As an educator, I had to figure out a way to meet them in the middle and in the process still have an influential effect with regard to their academic careers as novice, intermediate, and skilled researchers. In doing so, it became clear that using Hip Hop as a content source to help teach the research process was the appropriate method to introduce Information Literacy. In fall 2014, I created a 16-week curriculum - Hip Hop Information Literacy and introduced it to the library faculty.

*"Hip-hop is storytelling."* — Raquel Cepeda

## Hip Hop Information Literacy Case Study

To make a case for a new Hip Hop Information Literacy course a personal assessment of the university culture was recorded during my first year on campus. The quantitative measurements as a faculty member were obtained from an ACRL Assessment in Action Project Institutional Profile, a collaborative project completed by university faculty members, library faculty, and students (ACRL, 2015-2016). The qualitative information was based off observational experiences in the general information literacy course offering that I taught the first semester in the library. Students are not required to take an Information literacy course when they enroll as freshmen at this institution. With enrollment under 5,000, it made sense to step into a new realm and create an engaging collaborative environment for learning in the library.

## Quantitative: HBCU University Logistics

- Public Institution
- 1890-Land Grant Institution
- 150 years in existence
- Only university in the city populous
- Based in the state capitol - population 50,000
- Student Enrollment: 2,000 - 4,999 (FTE)
- Student Ethnic Population: | 50% White | 30% Black | 20% Other Ethnicities
- Faculty Ethnic Population: | 60% White | 15 % Black | 25% Other Ethnicities

## Qualitative: HBCU University Information

- All freshmen are required to take a GE101 course
- Students are reluctant to read
- Library Science Minor offered at institution
- Information Literacy not a required course for any academic major
- Freshmen in the past two years have only completed 1-2 semesters
- Students are more eager to join fraternal organizations versus educational

*"I've got a lot to teach but even more to learn."* - Atmosphere

## Creating: Hip Hop Information Literacy

In order to gain support for Hip Hop Information Literacy, a new definition regarding the subject matter had to be established. As a scholar, I wanted to make sure that the information aligned with the A.C.R.L. Frameworks for Information Literacy. In order to create a program of this caliber, the curriculum had to be based off a design that acknowledged knowledge practices adaptable to any major. According to the frameworks (2016), "Knowledge practices are the proficiencies or abilities that learners develop as a result of their comprehending a threshold concept" (ACRL, 2016, n. 5). Equally important, the cultural component that Hip Hop brings to the table when reinventing the wheel as it pertains to teaching and developing life-long learners that are a part of this movement. Creating a student survey, website, and an online lib. guide were additional elements that helped with the buy-in (as it pertains to faculty members and students).

## Definition: Hip Hop Information Literacy

Hip Hop Information Literacy is comprised of a group of knowledge practices that are necessary for students in an academic setting; in the information-digital age, students in an academic setting have to be cognizant of finding, retrieving, evaluating, applying, and acknowledging cultural, visual, and data literacy. The methodology is based on the Association of College & Research Libraries (A.C.R.L.) Framework for Information Literacy for Higher Education that uses its core concepts for literacy, and research, and has been implemented with flexible options by adhering to large ways of understanding within a discipline or unconventional setting.

## Outcomes: Academic-Collaborative Knowledge Participants

*Reading & Writing*

Students will be introduced to one author per semester and have the opportunity to discuss their perceptions and critical analysis through writing.

*Library & Research*

Students will become familiarized with the University Library, learn how to use online databases and cite information by activities based off instruction in a digital media environment.

*Creativity & Technology*

Students will create an online final project and upload their works to the university library repository.

*Information Literacy Think-Tank*

Students will utilize the skills they have learned to master and think critically within a group setting on a weekly basis.

## Elements: Survey, Website, Lib. Guide

*Course Pre-Survey*

The purpose of the initial survey is to assess student's knowledge about Hip Hop Information Literacy and general information for qualitative statistics about course demographics each semester. View Online: http://rebrand.ly/hiphoinfolitpresurvey

*Course Post-Survey*

The purpose of the exit survey is to assess student's learning progression during the semester and to allow them to have the opportunity to express their personal thoughts about the course and environment. View Online: http://rebrand.ly/hiphopinfolitpostsurvey

*Hip Hop Information Literacy Curriculum*

The curriculum for this course consists of the history about Hip Hop, the purpose of Hip Hop Information Literacy, a blueprint for academic success in the course, lecture series, and course resources. View Online: http://rebrand.ly/hiphopinfolitblueprint

*Hip Hop Information Literacy Website*

The website was created to allow students to access the course during the semester on their own terms. It is an interactive resource that features news regarding hip-hop, reading lists, course lectures and lessons. View Online: www.hiphopinformationliteracy.wordpress.com

*Hip Hop LibGuide*

The libguide has been developed to engage novice, intermediate, and skilled learners that are interested in learning more about the culture, social issues, and artistic components of Hip Hop. Students are encouraged to use the resource in class. View Online: www.hiphoplibguide.xyz

The Hip Hop Information Literacy course presents students with the opportunity to engage in a collaborative environment by using online resources and designated time to discuss current Hip Hop issues. Through the process, knowledge-participants are required to read, write, research on their own, utilize technology, and share work with their peers. Creating a course of this caliber has been a labor of love. I decided to go forth with my idea because I saw a need for students to be educated in their current moment/movement. Times are different and as educators, we must acknowledge this to make a difference in their lives. Expressing who you are and how you learn is important to students; using Hip Hop, a popular movement I share with my students, validates what they know, and acknowledges what I know, so we can learn from each other. This course is designed to encourage students to appreciate the importance of culture and diversity; in addition, this course is designed for students to develop the ability to think for themselves. Using the visual aesthetics and data-driven statistics of Hip Hop culture allows knowledge participants to see how the art form has changed over the years, and where they fit in the movement.

As a thought leader, choosing to create this course meant that I also had to be honest with myself about what I had observed and learned from students when I first started teaching Information Literacy. They professed often that they did/do not like to read. How in the world was I going to tackle this implication? In the journal article, Report on Information Literacy and the Mic: Teaching Higher Education Students Critical Research Skills Using Hip Hop Lyricism, Dara Walker (2008) reveals, "Undergraduate students have become accustomed to automation, reversing the ability to do basic hand work such as understanding the Library of Congress catalogue system and the use of microfiche and microfilm. Some students also find it difficult to work with indexes and databases" (Walker, 2008, p. 18). With that being said, I decided to assign students to read one book a semester in the course syllabus. From my viewpoint as a librarian, this was the only way that they would understand the importance of literacy and choosing to recommend works that have to deal with Hip Hop makes it more intriguing.

Equally important, if students cannot comprehend the information then they will not be able to complete the lessons or engage collaborative sessions or in conversation with their peers. My goal is to change the scope of how students interact with the material, become better researchers, and be able to acknowledge Hip Hop from a cultural standpoint through their writing and conversation.

*"Life without knowledge is[,] death in disguise"* - Black Star

## The 411: My Personal Analysis

The major premise behind Hip Hop Information Literacy is acknowledging culture and its significance in higher education. How can we educate students if we do not try to understand their everyday vernacular, style of dress, and music? I am not here to say that Hip Hop does not have its flaws, but it is a major cultural movement that has transformed the lives of many in our society. As I began to introduce students to Hip Hop Information Literacy, they seem to take it all in fast. I had to adjust the curriculum from 16-week lectures and scaled them down to 12 (though the course is still registered for 16 weeks); and hone in on the importance of understanding the reasoning behind why it is important to be a skilled researcher through each lesson. In the beginning, the uphill battle was daunting due to students not wanting to read the assigned course readings. I had talks with knowledge participants that enrolled in the course about the importance of literacy. It still feels like each semester I have to reiterate the importance of reading and the lifelong effects it has in making one a well-rounded individual and critical thinker.

It is quite interesting to me that black students and African American faculty are minorities even at an HBCU. To counteract this statistic, it was important to acknowledge their place in history as poets, artists, writers, Dj's, etc., and expose them to their own cultural brilliance. The Hip Hop movement began as a form of protest and social justice, just like the Black Arts Movement and the Civil Rights Movement. In like manner, it makes sense to share that information with students and then allow them the opportunity to share their own knowledge with their peers and instructor. Meeting 21st century knowledge participants where they are is the only way that we will be able to reach them going forward. This chapter was not written to give voice to a myriad of scholars and their assessment about Hip Hop. I wanted to share my own personal experience as a scholar with this audience in hopes of showing that Hip Hop is an educational incubator that has helped teach and train students to become intermediate and skilled researchers and learners. In designing this course, the unconference approach was the most helpful model for Hip Hop Information Literacy to come into fruition; I am still analyzing the curriculum, readjusting the course, and believe that it will be sound and succinct in a few more semesters.

Through this experience, I have learned as an educator that you have to be honest with your observations – they matter. It is important to have a good eye and to form relationships with students and faculty members to hear about how they have evaluated their institution, library, and the experiences that they have individually. As an instructor, I embrace their movement and want to learn more about it from their perspective, all the while showing them how to think critically and have the capability to research, write, and cite properly as future scholars in academia. We live in a collaborative society, and the route that I designed helped students become skilled at finding, retrieving, and acknowledging information through Hip Hop. Academic Librarians have the capacity to view their institutions from several lenses: culture-keepers; research scholars; information architects; curators of the arts; and, as community liaisons. Our job as instructors is to survey the university community and to share services and resources that will help them move forward as academic scholars and life-long learners.

# Using Technology to Communicate, Educate and Empower Girls of Color (GOC)

Loida Garcia-Febo
President, Information New Wave
International Library Consultant

## Introduction

Libraries and library associations are developing resources to encourage the use of technologies to communicate, educate, and empower girls from diverse ethnic groups. In order to identify best practices and recommendations, the author interviewed librarians serving girls of color and reviewed initiatives from various library associations.

During the United Nation's Second annual Multi-stakeholder Forum on Science, Technology and Innovation for the Sustainable Development Goals (SDGs), the United Nations Secretary, Ban Ki-Moon (2016), indicated that technologies are crucial to deliver the SDGs. SDGs are 17 aspirational goals established by the members of the U.N. and used by countries to guide their national development plans (2016). Global organizations such as the Bill and Melinda Gates Foundation's Global Libraries promote the use of technology and innovation to educate and empower women and girls in various regions of the world including Africa, Asia and the USA (1999, 2016). By using technologies, women can improve their farming, mothers can read, and potentially prevent childbirth mortality and they can start their own businesses.

According to the National Center for Women in Information Technology, the U.S. Department of Labor estimates that by 2020 there will be more than 1.4 million computing-related job openings. At current rates, however, we can only fill about 30% of those jobs with U.S. computing bachelor's grads. Girls represent a valuable, mostly untapped talent pool (2012).

In the USA, organizations such as Latina Girls Code, established in 2014, are working to bring new opportunities for Latina girls by aiming to fill the diversity gap between girls who are interested in technology through education and resources (2016). Black Girls Code was created in 2011 with alike goals, believing that the services provided by the organization will help to develop a true love for technology and the self-confidence that comes from understanding the greatest tools of the 21st century (2016).

Therefore, it is beneficial for our profession and our communities that we share recommendations and best practices from librarians serving girls of color to develop programming, provide access, and stay updated while using technology to communicate, educate, and empower girls of color.

## Programming Technology for Girls in Libraries

Best practices followed by Candice Mack, Senior Young Adult Librarian at Los Angeles Public Library, to develop successful programming include carrying out a community needs assessment, building partnerships with your local schools and other youth serving organizations to get to know the lay of the land and what the local needs and assets are and how the library can help fill any gaps. Connecting with those organizations is also a great way to get the word out about the library's resources and help facilitate partnerships among everyone in the community.

This type of assessment uncovers issues limiting access such as the lack of transportation of some POC patrons. L. Brown, a public librarian from Rhode Island, has seen how this is a significant factor for some girls in her service population. If the girls do not live in a place where they can walk to a library, they depend on the adults in their life to provide transportation. If the adults in their life work during the day, it can be difficult to bring these young women into the library.

Brown, who maintains ongoing communication with her community, also finds that many GOC are responsible for younger siblings during the afterschool hours. Many of their programs have age limits that prevent younger siblings from attending. Increasing the number of programs with wide age ranges have helped the library to help these girls take care of their siblings and attend programs. In their experience, they find parents are also more willing to provide transportation if more than one of their children can participate in the program, therefore they consider this an important best practice for reaching GOC.

Partnering with organizations has been fruitful for Brown. Her library has had success partnering with organization that already serve these girls, notably their local 21st Century afterschool program which is very diverse. That organization has exemplary high school students in leadership positions in the organization, and there are fewer transportation issues because the program happens at the school kids already attend. Brown says they have had a successful partnership with them, so she considers it a best practice to partner with organizations that are trusted by GOC and that put them in leadership positions.

In order to close the digital divide among her students, Valarie Husinger, a school librarian in the South Bronx, has also relied heavily on partnerships. Access to these essential technologies and exposure to new technologies is an essential first step. Everything she have been able to do to support her students is possible through partnerships. Just a few months ago, through a partnership with the New York City Department of Education, Husinger was able to get a brand new smart board for her school library which will help her teach digital skills, new headphones, and an ELMO, which allows you to project your physical writing or books. Partnerships are key to closing this digital divide for our girls. She believes that these efforts help us to teach the necessary knowledge and skills for digital tools.

In Hunsinger's experience, sometimes libraries are the only place for internet access. She believes that the role of libraries is fundamental to closing the digital divide for girls of color. Libraries can create a love for technology, which she gets to see every day. An important component of technology instruction is providing students with the opportunity to learn the skills not to just to use technology but that will allow them to participate in the creation of technology.

In her view, one of the most popular opportunities is coding. Last year 150 of her students in 4th and 5th grade participated in An Hour of Code made possible by Code.org which was key to teach students. This was one of their favorite experiences of the whole year. She found out that learning to code is one of the most in-demand opportunities. So, this year she is implementing a program called Girls Who Code, which is a free afterschool program that allows girls to explore coding. In this program, girls will not only develop skills but will build confidence. In after school programs we are also implementing maker spaces which will allow our students to explore low to high tech creation opportunities.

An ever-expanding digital universe will bring a higher value to information literacy skills such as basic reading and competence with digital tools. People who lack these skills will face barriers to inclusion in a growing range of areas. Through regular instruction, as well as an after-school technology club, technology skill levels have greatly improved in Hunsinger's school, along with a passion for technology. Technology instruction and integration have supported curriculum goals by incorporating the Empire State Information Fluency Continuum from the New York City Library System and has allowed students to create multimedia projects that will prepare them for 21st-century demands as specified in AASL's Standards for the 21st-Century Learner.

Public librarians who, like Mack, try to provide opportunities for girls of color at their library systems, might be interested in following her concept of Teen Tech Programming, whether it be through teaching teens and tweens how to create a radio show/podcast, hosting a program on how teens can get involved in local high school robotics teams, hosting a chipthrash concert (where the performers used hacked Gameboys to create music), workshops on learning how to solder (taught by a then 11 year old girl), and hosting a talk by a female engineer from NASA's Jet Propulsion Laboratory who has worked on the recent Mars Rover missions.

## Access For Girls

There are librarians like Mack who feel very fortunate that her community, library system and city are very supportive of serving girls from underserved populations. However, Mack thinks that the largest barriers to filling the diversity gap among those interested in technology are information and access. There are a lot of stereotypes about who "should be" or "can be" interested in technology. This may be caused by the lack of information provided to library users, beliefs that certain things are for boys and not for girls and limited access to computers or even mobile phones.

Husinger thinks school libraries can help motivate girls of color by teaching technology skills at a young age, thereby giving them  the confidence needed to pursue further education. She is dedicated to providing technology instruction as soon as possible, especially for those who lack access at home. This desire to help children, reflects Johnston's finding supporting school libraries being inherently linked to children's first use of technologies and how we should plan to reach all students (2012).

Librarians in Rhode Island have experienced mixed reactions to their programs. They have noticed that when they advertise youth technology programs, particularly Minecraft programs, parents are at times reluctant to sign up girls unless they know other girls will be at the program. Brown usually tells them, "I'm a girl!" since she will be offering the program. She is uncomfortable giving information about who else is signed up, and the truth is that she never knows for sure who will attend, so it is hard to answer the question otherwise.

Therefore, Brown believes the biggest barrier for girls to access technology is expressed through the question itself. The fact that parents think the program isn't a "girl thing" and through their actions send that message to their daughters. On the other hand, it also highlights the fact that parents are worried about their children, particularly GOC, feeling alone or singled out at a program. This is an understandable concerns that could be very difficult to address. A way to address concerns from parents could be through a one-page sheet with information about the events, the presence of a librarian during them, and examples of successful women of color in tech.

The most important thing libraries can do, Brown says, is put GOC in leadership positions around technology. They have many exemplary teen volunteers, including GOC who update laptops, assist with programs, and travel to other locations to help librarians demonstrate their 3D printers. For instance, one young woman even had her technology project featured in the library's annual report. The library provides volunteer training and does not require previous knowledge of specific technology, and as a result, they have had many GOC teaching younger children how to use their laptops, tablets, cameras, robots, and 3D printers. Brown believes that putting girls in these roles can change how they see themselves--not to mention, give them concrete experience they can put on a resume or a college application.

Libraries can have a significant role in filling the diversity gap between girls who are interested in technology through education and resources. Mack understands that by connecting teens, especially underserved teen girls, to technology education and resources in a non-threatening, non-graded manner like in the library is a great, low-pressure way to introduce all learners to a world that they might not otherwise be privy to due to lack of resources at home and at school.

As a school librarian working in the South Bronx, Husinger shares this view. She is driven to promote equitable accesses to technology while teaching the skills that will empower girls to take advantage of these jobs and opportunities in the tech field. She believes that librarians must act as equity warriors, working to close the resource and skills gap. Husinger has seen the difference between those we have never been online, who have never touched a computer and those who have the computer skills. Just a few months ago a student she works with shared a success story with her. Because the student had a professional email, knew how to type and composed an excellent email, she was able to receive a scholarship to a program. She had seen the student go from being able to type 4 words per minute to being able to create PowerPoints, Excel spreadsheets, and even coding.

## Staying Updated

Hunsinger believes that librarians may be the only trained person that students can go to for free technology help. Therefore, up-to-date trainings for librarians are critical to provide the best service for our patrons. Additionally, she says, it would be ideal if librarians could also train teachers on new technology opportunities so technology opportunities can reach students.

In Mack's view, it is also helpful to build and maintain relationships with other library systems as well as partner with youth-serving and technology organizations and companies outside of the library world to stay abreast of the evolving trends in technology, technology education and resources, to make sure that the information and resources that teens are encouraged to explore are both relevant to their needs as well as relevant and impactful to skill-building and jobs that they may seek in the future, and so that libraries are not unnecessarily re-inventing the wheel. Collaboration with other libraries is important for Mack and that is why she wanted to showcase the awesome, innovative and impactful work that many of the YALSA members are already doing. So that others could consider replicating the programs in their communities.

Library associations are moving forward to coordinate initiatives calling for more inclusive services. Mack's YALSA Presidential Initiative, 3-2-1 IMPACT! Inclusive and Impactful Teen Library Services received wide support from YALSA members (2015). Her call to action encouraged members to look at their communities and their capacity and see how to best align or realign their resources to make the most impact on the most vulnerable teen populations including unserved girls in their community, said Mack. As part of the initiative, a guide including programs for teens was developed and is available on the YALSA website (2016). Topics include coding, hip hop therapy, accessible gaming for the blind and visually impaired, STEM, and a model to link pregnant and parenting teens with resources.

Along with this effort, other ALA Divisions such as the Children and Technology Committee of the Association for Library Services to Children (ASCLA) continuously identify technology issues to inform members about how to enrich their programs and services. Library workers serving GOC can monitor ASCLA's blog to stay updated (2016). This past August, the Public Library Association released findings of a research in partnership with the Harvard Family Research Project which confirms that libraries are indeed creating new ways to serve all families and their children in our society which includes girls of color (2016). Libraries have a central space in communities and as such are positioned to engage families in learning processes.

School librarians like Hunsinger have the opportunity to work with a library advisory committee composed of students, teachers, and staff that allow her to identify and secure funding to move from four old computers to twenty-seven new machines. For many who don't have access to technology at home, these computers provide an essential lifeline, opening a world of opportunity. They also acquired an eReader, which many have used for the first time ever, allowing them to experience reading digitally. Most excitingly, her students have loved trying virtual reality for the first time and many asked how they can begin to make their own videos.

These types of experiences encourage Hunsinger to continue thinking that at the most basic level we must provide technology access to patrons. As a school librarian, she has fought to give her students the best technology possible because she believes that school libraries play an important role in bridging the digital divide or connectivity gap that separates various demographic groups, especially girls of color.

Also, on that front, the Los Angeles Public Library's (LAPL) Full STEAM Ahead initiative, which came out of Mack's Teen Tech Week work and a partnership between LAPL and the Discovery Science Center, is a great example of building the capacity of staff in STEAM skills in order to support them in helping to build STEAM skills in kids and teens.

## Conclusion

Although there are barriers such as those mentioned by our interviewees including the notion that technology is not for girls, limit to access, transportation, and girls tasked with adult chores, our interviewees shared recommendations to communicate, educate and empower girls of color GOC. Empathy is key to communicate with parents and girls, explaining processes and why it would benefit girls to learn about technology. It is also vital to make time for listening to girls which is a recommendation we can hear throughout the experiences shared by these librarians. Promoting girls' leadership in tech, connecting with other library systems to learn from one another, working with a library advisory board, staying up-to-date with technology to help patrons and students, using resources developed by library associations and the city's library system are recommendations to further the education of girls. Best practices to consider when developing programs to empower GOC involve being creative and flexible to adapt programming according to the girls' needs, persevering in coordinating initiatives, assessing community needs, and partnering with community groups and organizations.

The author would like to thank Candice Mack, M. Brown, and Valarie Hunsinger for their significant contributions to this paper.

figure 7

# Lowriders in Space: How a Graphic Novel Built a Community

Cathy Camper

## Abstract

Children's author and librarian Cathy Camper describes how she came up with the idea for her graphic novel Lowriders in Space in 2005 to help fill a dire need for more diversity in children's books. She shares how her goal for publishing Lowriders in Space and Lowriders to the Center of the Earth included bringing in another creator of color (Raúl III), and how their plan for their books reached beyond simply publishing, but extended to include building a community with the Latinx and Mexican American audience they hoped to reach, plus other targeted readers.

Some examples of how they've accomplished this include attending conferences like Reforma and Latino Comics Expo, connecting libraries and local lowriders groups via presentations at the library, so kids could learn STEM and local history via the cars and their creators, and sharing their experiences with other creators (kids and adults) to encourage them to "do-it-themselves."

Also, as an Arab American and Latino working together on this project, they aimed their books at where kids are now, living in the U.S., where kids' have an equal history of the old world, the world of U.S. pop culture, and a world of the many cultures of their friends.

**Lowriders in Space: How a Graphic Novel Built a Community**

I work as an outreach librarian, and I noticed that non-fiction books about lowriders got snapped up super fast when we did outreach at free lunch sites. I started to imagine another kind of book, a comic or graphic novel, one that would reach kids where they are now. I wanted something that would connect with English-Spanish speaking kids, because by 2050, the U.S. Census statistics said a third of the country would consist of English Spanish speaking households, and kids' books didn't reflect that. I wanted books that would appeal to boys, because boys' literacy rates were dropping. And I wanted it to be a graphic novel because I love comics and the way they use both writing and artwork to communicate. I couldn't help but include science in the books too, because there's so much to know about science in the everyday world, and STEM topics tie into school curriculum, which would make the books attractive to teachers and school librarians.

To truly create more diversity in children's books, the world of children's book creators and publishers needs to be more diverse too. So part of my plan was to use whatever writing skills and knowledge of publishing I had, to bring in another creator of color with me. In comics, it's common for artists and writers to collaborate. But in the world of children's books it's rare, and I got push back along the way for doing this. Raúl III is an extremely talented fine artist, but publishers were hesitant to take risks, especially during the last recession, when we were submitting our pitch. "Great writing, great art; too marginal an audience," one rejection told us. "Not quite right (i.e. white enough, I guessed) for us," another explained. We were fortunate to publish our book with Chronicle, where our editor Ginee Seo, who is Korean American, understood what we were trying to do. She wrote us an acceptance letter sharing that she was thrilled to publish a book like ours, because as an editor, she was finally in a position to change things by publishing books in which kids could see themselves, unlike the children's books she herself grew up with.

Also – very important – Raúl and I wanted to create a book that picked up on the mix of what kids are living right now in the U.S. Most kids' books are written by adults, and consciously or not, the stories often record what the adult author remembers from their childhood, what the adult author wants to pass on to young readers, as well as elements of the author's old world and/or the culture the author wants to preserve and protect. While all of these are important elements of books, Raúl and I purposely wanted to write a book that reflected the blend of where kids live today, a mix of the old world and new, Spanish and English, lowriders and rocket parts, Posada influenced art drawn with ballpoint pens any kid might own. Reviewers recognized that this unique quality made our books especially appealing to second and third generation Latinx. As Lowriders in Space says itself, "It's old – and new. It's retro-nuevo cool!"

We also aimed our books at a wide readership, while striving to keep the language, setting, look (including food and dress) culturally authentic. A glossary made Spanish words, car terms and science concepts understandable to kids without access to dictionaries, the Internet or helpful adults, for example, incarcerated and at risk youth. A respectful and mature sensibility made the book attractive to youth reading below grade level and ESL students, and notes at the back of the book shared more information about lowrider history, for those new to the culture. The story in our book, and our own approach to its creation both celebrate do-it-yourself culture, where using and sharing skills and working with friends lead to building things you love.

Unlike most artists and writers in children's books, Raúl and I came in as a partnership, so we were able to communicate with each other, and to riff off of each other's ideas like jazz musicians. Along with Chronicle, we worked to create a book with depth, that kids could pour over, laugh at and read multiple times -- a work of art that could be delivered to them by the turn of the page.

And so this book is also the collaboration of a Latino artist and an Arab American writer, something that addresses another U.S. Census prediction, that the fastest growing ethnicity in the U.S. is multi-racial. How future generations identify will be very different from the way people identify today. Our book looks towards a future where multi-racial and multiethnic creation is recognized and successful, much as the characters in the book build their car, but also as Raúl and I created these books.

Although I'd taken a few community college Spanish courses, I'm not fluent in Spanish. So I did tons of research - reading, watching films, going to lowrider car shows, and specifically listening and talking to Latinx about lowrider culture. Even more important than academic research for this book was listening to what people said. I'm grateful for all the help, support and comments I've had from Latinx friends, and the conversations we've had about both language and culture. I was writing outside my culture, so I tried to emulate what journalist do to convey stories outside of their backgrounds. I tried (and try) to shut up and listen, humble myself, put my writer's ego aside, and write respectfully. Although Raúl is Latino, he too needed to do research on cars and lowrider culture. The result of this research was that before our book even existed, a community grew up around it, and around both Raúl and I.

One of my dreams when I first wrote the book, was that someday there might be a way to get a non-profit to donate copies of our books to give out to families at lowrider car shows. When I attended a national lowrider show sponsored by Lowrider Magazine, the large number of families attending impressed me (the cost of an adult ticket wasn't cheap – but kids got in free). Still, my librarian self was saddened by the lack of any published material available at the show. How cool would it be for every family to get a full color graphic novel when they came to the show, honoring the culture they were creating? To provide a fun gift book fathers might read with sons, without heavy messages about literacy, schooling or rules, seemed like the ideal of how literacy should work.

Although this has yet to happen, I also thought of a way it might work in libraries, instead of at car shows. What if libraries could bring me or Raúl, to do presentations about our books and making zines and comics, and at the same time, the library could connect with local lowrider car clubs, to bring some cars to exhibit for kids to see? Public libraries bring big trucks to their spaces for kids to explore, and to promote STEM and maker space values. Bringing lowriders could do that, and more. Ideally, car owners could provide information and history about their rides, sharing car skills, local history and culture with a younger generation. The teachings, role models and creative initiative would then come from the community, with the library acting as facilitator, information retainer and resource.

To do this, I'd need to connect to Latinx librarians, and so I attended REFORMA's national conference, which was held in San Diego in 2015. I also wanted to attend the American Library Association's annual conference in the same year, because it was being held in San Francisco, and California is a key state for all things lowrider.

At Reforma, I presented a workshop called DiverZineties, which taught educators and librarians how to make zines to increase self-esteem and self-expression in teens, or other populations educators might serve. Through this workshop and others I attended, I connected with librarians and library workers on the West Coast, to share information about my book, and to brainstorm how an author tour might work.

When I attended ALA later that year, I was able to connect with librarians I'd met or been referred to at REFORMA, to plan a Bay Area author tour at libraries in the fall of 2015. I worked with librarians Laurie Willhalm (Oakland Public Library), Michelle Santamaria (Sebastopol Regional Library), and Mary Massa and Maricela Leon-Barrera (Mission District Library, San Francisco Public Library), as well as other library staff at each location, to put our plan into action. My agenda included book presentations and workshops making zines and mini-comics at five Oakland Public library branches, the Sebastopol library, and the Mission District Library on 24th and Mission Streets, the original lowrider neighborhood in San Francisco. My publisher added some school visits, a podcast interview and a bookstore signing. Oakland also brought in some classes from local schools to attend my visits at their Martin Luther King Jr. and César E. Chávez branch locations.

At each location, librarians tried to connect with local lowrider clubs to bring cars to exhibit. Unbeknownst to us, many of the clubs were participating in car shows that week, so they weren't able to help out libraries. In the end, only the Mission District was able to bring a car. They connected with Roberto Y. Hernandez, who, though he had engagements to attend to, agreed to leave his immaculate white 1964 Chevy Impala convertible parked in front of the library for a couple of hours, as long as we agreed to watch it. Branch librarian Maricela Leon-Barrera and I stood outside, handing out library fliers and Lowriders in Space bookmarks, keeping our eyes on his car.

Roberto wasn't there to share information, so my dream of sharing the history and technology of the cars didn't quite come about — at least, not the way I'd planned. But plenty of people stopped to admire his car. A couple out taking engagement photos posed in front of it. Many people who'd never set foot inside a library stopped to talk to us, and learned more about what the library could offer them. Others shared personal stories from the past, even remembering specific cars and their owners, from back in the day, when 24th and Mission was the center of lowrider cruising.

"If you ever want to draw attention to your library, park a lowrider in front of it," Maricela observed. We ran out of handouts, but were excited to have shared resources with folks who shared community stories with us. When Roberto returned several hours later to pick up his car, he hopped in and drove away, flanked by friends driving three other lowriders. To see a slow parade of those beautiful rides cruise once again through the Mission District was one of the best success stories I could have wished for. And I got to sit in that gorgeous car while it hopped! A real lowrider hopping is as good as I imagined it might be, when I first daydreamed about it, writing my book.

I share this story to share examples of how a book can instigate, inspire, connect with and build a community. But there are other examples. Reily Urban, a school librarian, shared this response of a fifth grade boy, after his class attended a Lowriders in Space presentation at his school:

He told his mom that day, "how this cool author came and showed a video of lowriders, and science books and drawings!" It was, "the best assembly he's seen on author days ever." He was also surprised their principal let the assembly be about lowrider culture.

Lowriders in Space has been out since 2014, and our second book Lowriders to the Center of the Earth came out July 2016. Now that the books exist, they're building community everywhere they go, with and without our direct input.

Attendees of my original zine workshops at Reforma and in the Bay Area have taken those zine skills to build other zine communities, to make zines with migrant workers, record stories of immigrants for archival collections and to start zine libraries in other public libraries. They've also worked with high school students to create zine exchanges, and they've encouraged student book clubs to share reviews of books they've read with other students, via zines.

In 2016, Lowriders to the Center of the Earth was awarded the 2016 Aesop Award from the American Folklore Society.  The award cited the book, saying:

For readers unfamiliar with the culture, it introduces them to a colorful new world yet one that has had significant impact on contemporary U.S. culture. Equally important, the Lowriders series celebrates the heritage of so many children growing up in the United States today. The fact that it is a graphic novel, the preferred genre of many younger readers, makes the story memorable and accessible.

When Raúl and I do presentations at schools, kids greet us by shouting out enthusiastically, "El Chavo!" when they recognize both Flapjack Octopus, and his hat, which pays tribute to El Chavo del Ocho, the popular Mexican TV show.  We have started to receive fan art (from both kids and adults), from as far away as Japan, from folks who've connected with our do-it-yourself message, drawing our characters with pencils and ballpoint pens.

Raúl has been invited to speak at WIDA National Conference for ESL teachers in Philadelphia, the MATSOL ESL conference in Massachusetts, the Sol Con in Columbus, Ohio, and in 2016, as a guest at the Latino Comics Expo at the Museum of Latin American Art in Long Beach, California. At the Expo, he was surprised by our first cosplay fans, a family whose son came to the Expo dressed as Flapjack Octopus. For Halloween, the whole Lozano family dressed up as the three Lowrider heroes, wearing lovingly made costumes that exemplified the do-it-yourself ethic our books share.

Educators have built creative lesson plans around the books too. Tiffany Coulson, who works for the non-profit Northwest Learning and Achievement Group in Washington State, helped plan this event:

The kids in our 95% Hispanic community will be designing mini cars this summer and will race them in August at a family STEM event. The police will be there with radar to clock their speed and give out "tickets" to the fastest cars! The facilitator will have guests that build custom low riders at the event for families to see. Can't wait!

In October 2015, Lowriders in Space was nominated for a Texas

Bluebonnet Award. Every year, fifteen books are nominated. Students must read at least five books to vote, which they do in January. In 2015, 100,000 students voted; what Texas does, Texas does big.

In October 2016, Raul and I did a whirlwind tour of four Texas cities, visiting schools and libraries to talk up our book. Raul visited several schools in Midland, Texas. But his visit also included The Hispanic Cultural Center of Midland, which presented a lowrider car show at Centennial Library, and featured a private reception, organized by the Midland Latino Cultural Center. It was attended by board members and organizers from the event. The food was delicious, enchiladas and other local dishes. In this way, Lowriders in Space isn't just a graphic novel; it's an extension and creator of a community, where the library, city residents, car clubs, cultural organizations and city dignitaries are all brought together because of a book.

But our book builds communities wherever it goes – even in neighborhoods that are more Anglo than Latinx. Laura Given, the school librarian at Parkview Center School in Roseville, Minnesota, invited me for an author visit for the third graders at their school. Their teachers worked with the students before my visit, reading Lowriders in Space and inventing creative activities based on the book. One teacher, Laura Dodge, wasn't able to attend my presentation, but told Laura Given Lowriders in Space had changed her classroom. I was curious what she meant, and asked if she could share with me what happened. Here is her reply:

> *Lowriders in Space transformed my classroom. This graphic novel helped me connect with the boys in my class, motivated non-readers, and helped to create a positive classroom community.*

At the beginning of the school year, my third grade boys and I were having a hard time connecting. I was looking up scores of games each morning to have something to talk about with this competitive group. Pretty soon, the lessons that developed because of Lowriders in Space had the kids lined up to talk to me what they had created. Students worked tirelessly on writing their own comic strips, in the artistic style of the illustrations in the book, using ballpoint pens. We even hosted a cosmic car contest of our own. Students drew and labeled their creations, and then orally defended why their car should be the winner of a car full of cash. (We used a toy car with a dollar strapped to the top.)

Sadly, many of my students would never have considered themselves a reader before reading this as a class. When we were introduced to Lowriders in Space by our librarian, the option of reading a graphic novel as an assignment in school was a thrill. Students developed such a deep understanding of the setting, plot and characters, they were able to make a timeline of the events in the book as a team. The kids couldn't get enough of the book, and were begging to read ahead, read it again, read the sequel, and now, to read other graphic novels.

Though most of the students in my class do not look like or come from a cultural background like the characters in this book, this book started a valuable conversation. My quiet Spanish-speaking students were proud to pronounce the words for the class.

The neighborhood the book is set in was a great starting point to a conversation about communities and how they may be similar and different from our own. Working as a team for the greater good, as the characters in this book did, became a theme for our classroom. Everyone has something they are good at and everyone should have a valuable contribution to our community. We are capable of anything when we talk and work together.

After reading Lowriders in Space, I had a deeper connection with the boys in my classroom because we had a common experience to talk about. All of my students are readers, and would now call themselves that. In fact, they began to devour books from our library's graphic novel section. Most importantly, this book helped to build a culture in our classroom community where different perspectives and talents are valued and used for the greater good.

If we are going to truly diversify children's books, the most successful books will be ones that reflect cultures truthfully, and that are written with respect and research. They will be books that bring more people of color into the creation process, and encourage and empower young readers of color to "do it themselves," whatever their hopes and dreams may be. Finally, they'll be books that build communities of support wherever they go, and by doing so, will lay new roads to success for future books by creators of color, which will create a wider, more truthful view of all the world's people in young readers' books.

Figure 8

figure 9

# Conclusion

Whew! For a first book--that was pretty damn fun, challenging, educational, stressful, rewarding and more! As we finish this book, the fascist state of the 45th president of the US is taking root. We hope our book serves as as a catalyst for more independent thinking, independent librarianship, innovative programming and independent publishing in the library/information field. So many of these topics are even more relevant now than when they were written a very short time ago. Whether it be the zine library that just lost it's funding, or the attack on ethnic caucuses of the ALA, or prison librarian issues, or the incorporation of Hip Hop into the curriculum, or Whiteness in libraries--these issues are today's challenges and demand attention, thought and solutions.

The spine bears the weight of our desire to make all those pages stick together. It's a berm of constant pressure, an infinite, miniscule tearing that never quite shears. The spine bears the weight of the book for the sake of the pages; the librarians we have been fortunate enough to showcase in this first volume are asking important questions and balking at convenient answers. They are going to listen to you, but not if what you come through with is tired, narrow-minded, and morose. At the same time, these librarians are not seeking your professional approval either; they are saying, look, this here has worked for me, it may work for you too, so take and choose what works for you. We are not here to trigger your sensibilities, or causes you to quiver in your cardigan, but we have come to ask the right questions.

Let's talk realistically about the inequalities in resources between affluent neighborhoods and those where people rent instead of own their own home. Let's address the inequalities in education and class before we cast stones or launch diatribes. Let's realize our privileges and understand our deficiencies and move forward with positive spirit and dutiful minds. Let's cultivate a compassion for knowledge and mistrial dubious bunkum.

**My thanks go out to our wonderful authors who contributed straight from their hearts and who indeed, all have spines!**

**Many thanks go out to those who contributed to our crowdsourcing campaign!  We could not have done this without you!**

**Thanks to you dear reader--we did this for you!**

Thanks especially to Autumn Anglin--who is a design genius, a workaholic, an artist extraordinaire, an amazing editor, proofer, writer, student, mother and friend.  This collaboration happened as it was meant to happen, just as these authors were meant to write these chapters and you were meant to read them.  Onward, keep the energy up and never stop fighting for progress!

Max Macias and Yago Cura

March, 2017

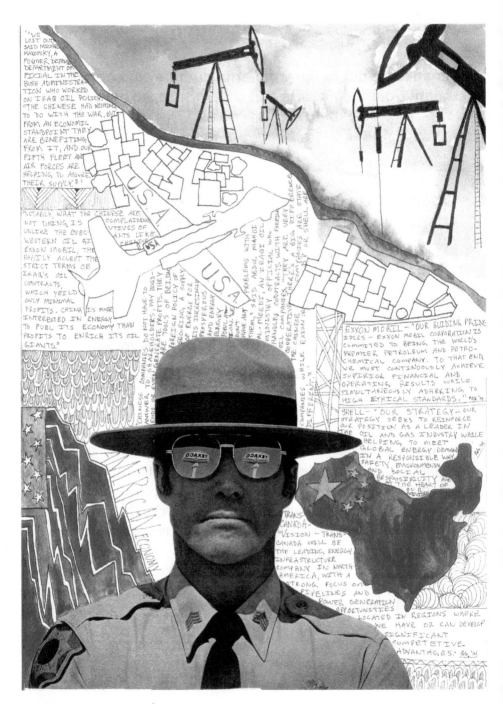

Figure 10

# Image Credits

Figure 1: *Built on Bones*. Digital Art. 2016.

Figure 2: *Your Reason*. Mixed Media. 2014.

Figure 3: *Imagine You're Enlightened*. Mixed Media. 2016.

Figure 4: *Question Everything*. Mixed Media. 2014.

Figure 5: *Past, Present, Future*. Mixed Media. 2012.

Figure 6: *He Him His*. Watercolor and Pen on paper. 2017.

Figure 7: *Feminist*. Mixed Media. 2016.

Figure 8: *Do You Understand?* Watercolor and pen on paper. 2014.

Figure 9: *We have to pee*. Mixed Media. 2016.

Figure 10 : *The Fall of America*. Mixed Media. 2014.

Figure 11: *People for sale*. Mixed Media. 2016.

Figure 12: *Animal Testing*. Mixed Media. 2014.

Figures reproduced with permission from the artist Autumn Anglin.

# Appendix A

Email Survey Fall, 2016: US State Library Entities "Does your state library entity provide monetary support to state prison libraries?"

| | | | |
|---|---|---|---|
| Alabama | no response | Montana | no |
| Alaska | no response | Nebraska | no |
| Arizona | no response | Nevada | no response |
| Arkansas | no response | New Hampshire | no |
| California | no | New Jersey | no response |
| Colorado | YES | New Mexico | no |
| Connecticut | no | New York | YES |
| Delaware | no | North Carolina | no |
| Florida | no | North Dakota | no |
| Georgia | no response | Ohio | no |
| Hawaii | no | Oklahoma | YES |
| Idaho | no | Oregon | no |
| Illinois | no | Pennsylvania | no |
| Indiana | no | Rhode Island | no |
| Iowa | no | South Carolina | no |
| Kansas | no | South Dakota | no |
| Kentucky | no response | Tennessee | no |
| Louisiana | no | Texas | no |
| Maine | no | Utah | no |
| Maryland | no response | Vermont | no |
| Massachusetts | no | Virginia | no response |
| Michigan | no | Washington | YES |
| Minnesota | no response | Washington DC | no response |
| Mississippi | no | West Virginia | no |
| Missouri | no response | Wisconsin | no response |
| | | Wyoming | YES |

figure 11

# References

## EXPERIENCING WHITENESS OF LIS EDUCATION: AN AUTOETHNOGRAPHIC ACCOUNT

Althusser, L. (1970). Ideology and ideological state apparatuses: Notes towards an investigation. Retrieved from https://www.marxists. org/reference/archive/ althusser/1970/ideology.htm

American Library Association. (2012). Diversity counts tables, 2012 update. [Data file]. Retrieved from http://www.ala.org/ offices/sites/ala.org.offices/files/ content/diversity/diversitycounts/ diversitycountstables2012.pdf

Anderson, L. (2006). Analytic autoethnography. Journal of Contemporary Ethnography, 35(4), 373-395. DOI: 10.1177/0891241605280449

Bales, S.E. & Engle, L.S. (2012). The counterhegemonic academic librarian: A call to action. Progressive Librarian (40), 16-40.

Berry, J. D. (2004). Back talk: White privilege in library land. Library Journal. [Web log]. Retrieved from http://lj.libraryjournal. com/2004/06/ljarchives/backtalk-white- privilege-in-library-land/#_

Bourg, Chris. (2014). The unbearable whiteness of librarianship. The feral librarian. [Web log]. Retrieve from https://chrisbourg.wordpress. com/2014/03/03/ the-unbearable-whiteness-of-librarianship/

Boylorn, R. M. & M. P. Orbe. (2014). Critical autoethnography as a method of choice. In R. M. Boylorn & M. P. Orbe (Eds.) Critical autoethnography: Intersecting cultural identities in everyday life (13-26). Walnut Creek, CA: Left Coast Press.

Calgary Anti-Racism Education Collective. (2015). Understanding whiteness. Retrieved from http://www.ucalgary.ca/cared/whiteness

Cann, C.N. & DeMeulenaere, E.J. (2012). Critical co-constructed autoethnography. Cultural Studies & Critcal Methodologies, 12(2), 146-158. DOI: 10.1177/1532708611435214

Daft, R.L. (2010). Management, 9th ed. Mason, OH: South-Western Cengage Learning.

Du Bois, W.E.B. (1986). The souls of black folk. In Huggins, N. (Ed.) W.E.B. Du Bois: Writings (357-548). New York: Library of America.

Ellis, C. & Bochner, A. P. (2003). Autoethnography, personal narrative, reflexivity: Researcher as subject. In N. K. Denzin & Y. S. Lincoln (Eds.) Collecting and Interpreting Qualitative Materials (199-258). Thousand Oaks, CA: Sage.

Ellis, C., Adams, T. E., & Bochner, A.P. (2011). Autoethnography: An overview. Forum Qualitative Sozialforschung / Forum: Qualitative Social Research, 12(1), article 10. Retrieved from http://nbn-resolving.de/um:nbn:114-fqs1101108

Galvan, A. (3 June 2015). Soliciting performance, hiding bias: Whiteness and librarianship. In the Library with a Lead Pipe. Retrieved from http://www.inthelibrarywiththeleadpipe.org/2015/soliciting-performance-hiding-bias-whiteness-and-librarianship/

Giroux, H.A. (1992). Critical pedagogy and cultural power: An interview with Henry A. Giroux. Border crossings: Cultural workers and the politics of education (149-160). Routledge: New York.

Giroux, H.A. (1997). Channel surfing: Racism, the media, and the destruction of today's youth. New York: St Martin's Press.

Gonzalez-Smith, I., Swanson, J. & Tanaka, A. (2014). Unpacking identity: Racial, ethnic, and professional identity and academic librarians of color. In. Pagowsky, N. & Rigby, M. (Eds.) The librarian stereotype: Deconstructing perceptions and presentations of information work (149-173). Chicago: ALA.

Green, M. J., Sonn, C. C., & Matsebula, J. (2007). Reviewing whiteness: Theory, research, and possibilities. South African Journal of

Psychology, 37(3), 389-419.

Hathcock, A. (7 Oct. 2015). White librarianship in blackface: Diversity initiatives in LIS. In the library with a lead pipe. Reteived from http://www.inthelibrarywiththeleadpipe.org/2015/lis-diversity/

Kim, K., & Sin, S. (2008). Increasing Ethnic Diversity in LIS: Strategies Suggested by Librarians of Color. The Library Quarterly: Information, Community, Policy, 78(2), 153-177. doi:1. Retrieved from http://www.jstor.org/stable/10.1086/528887 doi:1

Leonardo, Z. (2002). The souls of white folk: critical pedagogy, whiteness studies, and globalization discourse. Race Ethnicity and Education, 5(1): 29–50.

McIntosh, P. (1989). White privilege: Unpacking the invisible knapsack. Peace and Freedom Magazine, (July/August), 10-12. Retrieved from http://nationalseedproject.org/white- privilege-unpacking-the-invisible-knapsack

Pawley, C. (2006). Unequal legacies: Race and multiculturalism in the LIS curriculum. The Library Quarterly: Information, Community, Policy, 76(2), 149-168.

United States Census Bureau. (2010). 2008-2010 American Communities Survey. [Data file]. Retrieved from http://factfinder.census. gov/faces/tableservices/jsf/ pages/productview.xhtml?src=bkmk

Wall, S. (2006). An autoethnography on learning about autoethnography. International Journal of Qualitative Methods, 5(2), article 9. Retrieved from http://www.ualberta.ca/~iiqm/backissues/5_2/pdf/wall.pdf

---. (2008). Easier said than done: Writing an autoethnography. International Journal of Qualitative Methods, 7(1), (38-53). Retrieved from http://ejournals.library.ualberta.ca/ index.php/IJQM/article/viewFile/1621/1144

Witkin, S. L. (2014). Autoethnography: The opening act. In S. L. Witkin (Ed.) Narrating social work through autoethnography (1-24). New York: Columbia University.

ENGAGING THE FUTURE OF ZINE LIBRARIANSHIP

## Interviews

Cathy Camper, interview by author, Portland, OR, April 6, 2014.

Cathy Camper, interview by author, Portland, OR, May 07, 2014.

Jenna Freedman, interview by author, New York City, NY, March 27, 2014.

Jenna Freedman, interview by author, via video stream, May 06, 2014.

## Interview Questions

Interviewee Background

What is your name, position, institution?

Briefly describe your role within your library?

What motivates you to keep focusing upon zines in your librarianship? What are the benefits of zines as a medium for you as a librarian?

What are some differences and similarities between a zine librarian and a librarian?

## Institutional Perspectives

What is the strategy at this institution for improving the zine collection?

What resources are available to zine librarians from your institution? From elsewhere? What type of community is out there?

Have you or your colleagues encountered resistance to reforms in your zine library?

What should librarians who want to work with zines do to prepare to become involved with this work?

## Assessment

What do you use as evidence within your library to assess patron interest?

Where do you see your collection going in the next ten years?

## Challenges and Evaluation

What are the major challenges your department faces if there is an attempt to change the existing zine collection? What are the major opportunities?

What are the major hurdles involved in zine librarianship?

## Future of Zine Librarianship

Where do you think zine librarianship is headed?

What is the state of hiring of zine librarians for academic and public libraries?

What are some trends you've observed within zine culture, within zine librarianship, and within librarianship as a whole?

What is some advice you can give to LIS students with budding interests in independent comics, zines, and alternative ephemera?

What areas of zine librarianship do you think needs to be addressed in future research? Why is that?

## References

Bartel, J. (2004). From A to Zine: Building a Winning Zine Collection in Your Library. Chicago: American Library Association.

Berman, S. (1981). The Local Library and the Small Press. Small Press Review 13.6, 37-38.

Berman, S. & Danky, J.P (Eds). (1999) Alternative Library Literature, 1998/1999 A Biennial Anthology. Jefferson, North Carolina: McFarland & Company, Inc., Publishers.

Brager, J., & Sailor, J. (Eds.). (n.d.). Archiving the Underground [zine] (Vol. 1).

Chepesiuk, R. (2007). The Zine Scene: Libraries Preserve the Latest Trend in Publishing. American Libraries, 28(2), 68–70.

DesHarnais, M. (2006). A Miniguide. Library Journal, 39.

Dilevko, J. (2008). An Alternative Vision of Librarianship: James Danky and the Sociocultural Politics of Collection Development. Library

Trends, 56(3), 678–704.

Dodge, C. (2008). Collecting the Wretched Refuse: Lifting a Lamp to Zines, Military Newspapers, and Wisconsinalia. Library Trends, 56(3): 667-77.

Dodge, C. (2005, August). The New Monastic Librarians. UTNE. Retrieved from http://www.utne.com/community/the-new-monastic-librarians.aspx

Dodge, C. (1995). Pushing the Boundaries: Zines and Libraries. Wilson Library Bulletin, 69, 26–30.

Dodge, C. (2008). Taking Libraries to the Street: Infoshops and Alternative Reading Rooms. American Libraries, 62–64.

Duncombe, S. (2007). Notes From Underground: Zines and the Politics of Alternative Culture. New York: Verso Press.

Eichhorn, K. (2013). The Archival Turn in Feminism: Outrage in Order. Philadelphia: Temple University Press.

Freedman, J. (2008). AACR2-bendable but not flexible: cataloging zines at Barnard College. Radical Cataloging: Essays at the Front. Ed. K.R. Roberto. Jefferson, NC: McFarland & Co.

Freedman, J. (2009). Grrrl Zines in the Library. Signs: Journal of Women in Society and Culture, 35(1), 52–58.

Freedman, J. (2012). Lower East Side Librarian: Special Zine Tour Edition (3rd Edition.). New York City: J. Freedman.

Freedman, J. (2011). Pinko vs. Punk: A Generational Comparison of Alternative Press Publications and Zines. In The Generation X Librarian: Essays on Leadership, Technology, Pop Culture, Social Responsibility and Professional Identity. Edited by Martin K. Wallace, Rebecca Tolley-Stokes and Erik Sean Estep. Jefferson, N.C.: McFarland & Co.

Freedman, J. (2006). Your Zine Tool Kit, DIY Collection. Library Journal, 131(111), 36–38.

Get Involved. (n.d.). Retrieved August 4, 2014, from http://zinepavilion.tumblr.com/getinvolved

Gisonny, K., & Freedman, J. (2006). Zines in libraries: how, what and why? Collection Building, 25(1), 26–30.

Hays, A. (2011, January). An Interview with Jenna Freedman. storyscape literary journal. Retrieved from http://storyscapejournal.com/issue6/stories/an-interview-with-jenna-freedman.php

Herrada, J. (1995). Zines in Libraries: A Culture Preserved. The Balance Point, 21(2), 79–88.

Honma, T. (2016). From Archives to Action: Zines, Participatory Culture and Community Engagement in Asian America. Radical Teacher, 105: pp. 33-43.

Hubbard, C. (2005). DIY in the Stacks: A Study of Three Public Library Zine Collections. Public Libraries, 44(6), 351–354.

Koppel, L. (2006, April 11). Zines in the Library Catalogue? Of Course. The New York Times. NY Region.

Kucsma, J. (2002). Countering Marginalization: Incorporating Zines into the Library. Library Juice, 5(6), 1–15.

Licona, A. (2012). Zine in Third Space: Radical Cooperation and Borderlands Rhetoric. Albany: State University of New York Press.

Morgan, S., & Dawson, E.-J. (2010). Zine Scene at Multnomah County Library: An Interview with Emily-Jane Dawson. Oregon Library Association, 16(1), 21–25.

Murphy, R. E., Freedman, J., & Sellie, A. (Eds.). (2009). Zine Librarian Zine: DIY-IYL Do It Yourself in Your Library. New York City, NY.

Nelsen, S. (n.d.). Multnomah County Library Champions Portland Zine Scene. Oregon Library Association, 13(2), 17–19.

Nguyen, M.T. (2004). Race Riot Project Directory. Berkeley, CA: Self-published.

Perris, K. (2004). Unearthing the underground: a comparative study of zines in libraries (MA in Information Services Management). London Metropolitan University.

Piepmeier, A. (2009). Girl Zines: Making Media, Doing Feminism. New York City: New York University Press.

Singer, P., and Griffin, G. (2010). Succession Planning in the

Library: Developing Leaders, Managing Change. Chicago: American Library Association.

Solorzano, D.G. & Yosso, T. (2002) Critical Race Methodology: Counter-Storytelling as an Analytical Framework for Education Research. Qualitative Inquiry, 8, pp: 23-44.

Stoddart, R. and Kiser, T. (2004) Zines and the Library. Library Resources and Technical Services, 48(3), pp.191-198.

Tkach, D., & Hank, C. (2014). Before Blogs, There Were Zines: Berman, Danky, and the Political Case for Zine Collecting in North American Academic Libraries. Serials Review, 40(1), 12–20.

Vale, V. (1996). Zines! (Vol. 1). San Francisco, CA: Re/Search Publications.

Vale, V. (1997). Zines! (Vol. 2). San Francisco, CA: Re/Search Publications.

West, J. (2006). Life in the Trenches of Print and Web Publishing: An Interview with Jenna Freedman, Curator of the Barnard Zine Collection. Serials Review, 32, 266–269.

Woodbrook, R., & Lazzaro, A. (2013). The Bonds of Organization: Zine Archives and the Archival Tradition. Journal of Western Archives, 4(1), 1–18.

Wooten, K. (2015). Zine Librarians Code of Ethics Zine. Durham, NC: the authors.

Wrekk, A. (2003). Stolen Sharpie Revolution 2. Portland: Microcosm Publishing.

Zass, E. (2001). Underground Anthropologist: An Interview with Independent Publisher V. Vale. Clamor, 8, pp. 42-46.

Zine Librarian (un)Conferences - ZineLibraries.info. (n.d.). Retrieved from http://zinelibraries.info/events/zine-librarian-unconferences/

Zobel, Cheryl. (1999). Zines in Public Libraries. Counterpoise 3.2:

## THE IMPORTANCE OF LIBRARIAN ETHNIC CAUCUSES AND THE SLANDER OF "SELF-SEGREGATION"

American Indian Library Association. (2015, May 13). Dr. Loriene Roy receives AILA distinguished service award. Retrieved from http://ailanet.org/dr-loriene-roy-receives-aila-distinguished-service-award/.

American Library Association. (2012). Diversity counts 2009-2010 update. Retrieved from http://www.ala.org/offices/sites/ala.org.offices/files/content/diversity/diversitycounts/diversitycountstables2012.pdf.

Black Caucus of the American Library Association, Inc. (u.d.). Our history. Retrieved from http://bcala.org/our-history/#.

Bourg, C. (2014, March 3). The unbearable whiteness of librarianship. Feral Librarian. Retrieved from https://chrisbourg.wordpress.com/2014/03/03/the-unbearable-whiteness-of-librarianship/.

Bowie, N. (2007, February 12). 'Self-segregation' myth affects all student groups. Yale Daily News. Retrieved from http://yaledailynews.com/blog/2007/02/12/self-segregation-myth-affects-all-groups/.

Congressional Black Caucus Foundation, Inc. (2017). Learn about us. Retrieved from http://www.cbcfinc.org/learn-about-us/.

Gillborn, D. (2009). Education policy as an act of supremacy: Whiteness, critical race theory, and education reform. In E. Taylor, D. Gillborn, & G. Ladson-Billings (Eds.), Foundations of critical race theory in education (pp. 51-69). New York, NY: Routledge.

Johnson, T.R. (2016, April 28). The increasing irrelevance of the congressional black caucus. The Atlantic. Retrieved from http://www.theatlantic.com/politics/archive/2016/04/congressional-black-caucus-donna-edwards-black-lives-matter/480180/

Kaczynski, A. (2016, September 22). GOP rep. Steve King: congressional black caucus is the "self-segregating caucus". BuzzFeed News. Retrieved from https://www.buzzfeed.com/andrewkaczynski/gop-rep-steve-king-congressional-black-caucus-is-the-self-se?utm_term=.im4DAb9kXx#.lgeGneP1p7. \

Kurz, R. [robinkurz]. (2016, November 22). @BC_ALA Definitely (member of REFORMA longer than ALA), but > control by members & <

normalization of Whiteness +far < institutional inertia [Tweet]. Retrieved from https://twitter.com/robinkurz/status/801111063362146306.

Litwin, R. (2016, November 21). The ALA Washington Office press releases and Todaro's Monday morning misdirection (#NotMyALA). Library Juice. Retrieved from http://libraryjuicepress.com/blog/?p=5429.

McPherson, D. (2009, September 10). Alumna named first Hispanic president of American Library Association. University of Denver Magazine. Retrieved from https://magazine.du.edu/alumni/alumna-named-first-hispanic-president-of-american-library-association/.

National Association of Black Journalists. (u.d.) History/mission. Retrieved from http://www.nabj.org/?page=History.

Olivos, E.M. & Ochoa, A.M. (2008). Reframing due process and institutional inertia: a case study of an urban school district. Equity & Excellence in Education, 41(3) 279-292.

Simmons, J. (2016). Lawyers in libraries: FAMU law program report. BCALA News, 43(4) 9-10.

Tesfaye, S. (2017, January 11). Watch: congressional black caucus says Jeff Sessions' confirmation will set back the cause for universal civil rights. Salon. Retrieved from http://www.salon.com/2017/01/11/watch-congressional-black-caucus-says-jeff-sessions-confirmation-will-set-back-the-cause-of-universal-civil-rights/.

World Net Daily. (2015, September 11). Progressives become unglued over 'white' student unions. World Net Daily. Retrieved from http://www.wnd.com/2015/12/progressives-come-unglued-over-white-student-unions/.

Yale Daily News. (2007, February 9). Self-segregation thwarts campus unity. Yale Daily News. Retrieved from http://yaledailynews.com/blog/2007/02/09/self-segregation-thwarts-campus-unity/.

## I'M NOT A TOKEN: REFLECTIONS ON BLACK AND LATINX REPRESENTATION AND YOUTH SERVICES

Accapadi, Mamta Motwani. When White Women Cry: How White Women's Tears Oppress Women of Color. College Student Affairs Journal. Spring 2007. v26 n2 p208-215. Retrieved from http://files.eric.ed.gov/fulltext/EJ899418.pdf

Arrington, E. G., Hall, D. M., & Stevenson, H. C. (2003, Summer). The Success of African-American Students in Independent Schools. Independatn School Magazine. Retrieved from http://www.nais.org/Magazines-Newsletters/ISMagazine/Pages/The- Success-of-African-American- Students-in- Independent-Schools.aspx

Association of Library Services to Children (ALSC) 2016 Environmental Scan: The Current and Future State of Youth Librarianship 2016 ALSC Emerging Leader Team, June 10, 2016. Retrieved from ttp://www.ala.org/alsc/sites/ala.org.alsc/files/content/professional-tools/2016%20 ALSC%20Env%20Scan.pdf

DiAngelo, Robin. White Fragility. International Journal of Critical Pedagogy, Vol 3 (3) (2011) pp 54-70. Retrieved from http://libjournal.uncg.edu/ijcp/article/viewFile/249/116.

Diversity Counts Office for Research and Statistics Office for Diversity (Research Report No.39) (D. M. Davis & T. D. Hall, Comps.). (2012). Retrieved from ALA website:http://www.ala.org/offices/sites/ala.org.offices/files/content/diversity/diversitycounts/diversitycountstables2012.pdf

Kelley, M. (2013, May 23). The MLS and the Race Line [Editorial]. Library Journal. Retrieved from http://lj.libraryjournal.com/2013/05/opinion/editorial/the-mls- and-the- race-line/

Kelley, M. (2013, May 23). The MLS and the race line [Editorial]. Library Journal.

Library Workers: Facts and Figures. Department for Professional Employees. March 8, 2017. Retrieved from http://dpeaflcio.org/programs-publications/issue-fact-sheets/library-workers- facts-figures/

McCook, K. D. L. P. (1997, March 25). Planning for a Diverse workforce in Library and Information Science Profession [Table]. Retrieved from Eric database. (ED 402 948) statistical data

Mestre, Lori. Librarians Working with Diverse 3 Populations: What Impact Does Cultural 4 Competency Training Have on Their Efforts. The Journal of Academic Librarianship. November 2010. Retrieved from https://www.ideals.illinois.edu/bitstream/handle/2142/26006/ Mestre_librarians_working_with_diverse_populations_proof.pdf?sequence=2

Morris, M. W. (2016). Pushout: The criminalization of Black girls in schools. New York: The New Press.

Sue, D. W. (2010). Microaggressions in everyday life: Race, gender, and sexual orientation. Hoboken, N.J.: Wiley.

Thomas, D. A. (2001). The Truth about Mentoring Minorites, Race Matters. Harvard Business Review, 99-107.

Thomas, K. M., Willis, L. A., & Davis, J. (2007). Mentoring minority graduate students: issues and strategies for institutions, faculty, and studnets. Equal Oppertunities International, 26(3), 178-192.

Williams, T. (2016, May 31). Inclusivity in Any Library [Blog post]. Retrieved from American Libraries Magazine website: https://americanlibrariesmagazine.org/2016/05/31/inclusivity-accessibility- in-any- library/

## CRITLIB MANAGEMENT: LEADING AND INSPIRING THROUGH A SOCIAL JUSTICE FRAMEWORK

Bohyun, K. (2016, November 12). Say It Out Loud - Diversity, Equity, and Inclusion. Retrieved from http://www.bohyunkim.net/blog/archives/3587

Cone, J. (2004). Theology's Great Sin: Silence in the Face of White Supremacy. Black Theology, 2(2), 139–152. https://doi.org/10.1558/blth.2.2.139.36027

Cottrell, M. (2015, May 1). Baltimore's Library Stays Open During Unrest. Retrieved September 22, 2016, from https://americanlibrariesmagazine.org/blogs/the-scoop/qa-carla-hayden-baltimore/

Dickerson, C., & Saul, S. (2016, November 10). Campuses Confront Hostile Acts Against Minorities After Donald Trump's Election. The New York Times. Retrieved from http://www.nytimes.com/2016/11/11/us/police-investigate-attacks-on-muslim-students-at-universities.html

Human Rights Campaign. (2016). Violence Against the Transgender Community in 2016. Retrieved November 17, 2016, from http://www.hrc.org/resources/violence-against-the-transgender-community-in-2016/

Hussey, L. (2010). The Diversity Discussion: What are we saying? Progressive Librarian, (34–35), 3–10.

Libraries 4 Black Lives. (2016a). Ideas, Actions and More. Retrieved September 30, 2016, from http://libraries4blacklives.org/yourideas/

Libraries 4 Black Lives. (2016b). Take The Pledge. Retrieved November 17, 2016, from http://libraries4blacklives.org/pledge/

Mathuews, K. (2016). Moving Beyond Diversity to Social Justice: A Call to Action for Academic Libraries. Progressive Librarian, (44), 6.

Maxey-Harris, C., & Anaya, T. (2010). Diversity Plans and Programs, SPEC Kit 319 (October 2010). Retrieved from http://publications.arl.org/Diversity-Plans-and-Programs-SPEC-Kit-319/

Moreland, K., Nguyen, V., & Sadruddin, W. (2016, September). A conversation about diversity. Oregon College of Oriental Medicine.

Obear, K., & Kerr, S. (2015). Creating inclusive organizations: one student affairs division's efforts to create sustainable, systemic change. In S. K. Watt (Ed.), Designing Transformative Multicultural Initiatives: Theoretical Foundations, Practical Applications, and Facilitator Considerations (pp. 136–152). Sterling, VA: Stylus Publishing.

Peet, L. (2016, August 10). Public Librarians Launch Libraries4BlackLives. Retrieved November 14, 2016, from http://lj.libraryjournal.com/2016/08/people/public-librarians-launch-libraries4blacklives/

Reif, L. R. (2016, July 10). Letter from President Reif regarding recent violent tragedies in the United States. Retrieved September 30, 2016, from http://news.mit.edu/2016/letter-regarding-recent-violent-tragedies-0710

Stage, F. K., Muller, P., Kinzie, J., & Simmons, A. (1998). Creating Learning Centered Classrooms. What Does Learning Theory Have To Say? ASHE-ERIC Higher Education Report, Volume 26, No. 4. ERIC Clearinghouse on Higher Education, One Dupont Circle, N.W., Suite 630, Washington, DC 20036-1183; toll-free phone: 800-773-3742; fax: 202-452-1844. ($24). Retrieved from http://eric.ed.gov/?id=ED422778

Wall, V., & Obear, K. (2008). Multicultural Organizational Development (MCOD): Exploring Best Practices to Create Socially Just, Inclusive Campus Communities. Presentation at the American Association of Colleges and Universities Conference on Diversity, Learning, and Inclusive Excellence: Accelerating and Assessing Progress. Long Beach, CA. Retrieved from http://www.pdx.edu/sites/www.pdx.edu.studentaffairs/files/MCOD%20Best%20Practices2.pdf

Williams, M. (2016, October 6). White people don't understand the trauma of viral police-killing videos. Retrieved October 24, 2016, from http://www.pbs.org/newshour/updates/column-trauma-police-dont-post-videos/

## PRISON LIBRARIES: ON THE FRINGE OF THE LIBRARY WORLD

Allard, S. (2015, October 23). Placements & Salaries 2015: Salary by Library Type. Retrieved from http://lj.libraryjournal.com/2015/10/placements-and-salaries/2015-survey/salary-by-library-type/

California State Library, Communications. (2012, October 19). California State Library grant provides books [Press release]. Retrieved from http://www.library.ca.gov/pressreleases/pr_121019.html

Colorado Department of Education: Institutional Library Development. (n.d.). Retrieved November 14, 2016, from http://www.cde.state.co.us/cdelib/prisonlibraries/institutions

Colorado State Library. (n.d.). Institutional libraries: Impacting lives in meaningful ways [Brochure]. Author. Retrieved November 14, 2016, from http://www.cde.state.co.us/sites/default/files/documents/cdelib/prisonlibraries/download/pdf/ild_brochure.pdf

Connections. (2016). Connections 2016, 6-6. doi:10.17266/34

Correctional Services. (n.d.). Retrieved November 14, 2016, from https://www.nypl.org/help/community-outreach/correctional-services

Girmscheid, L., & Schwartz, M. (2014, July 3). Payday | LJ Salary Survey 2014. Retrieved from http://lj.libraryjournal.com/2014/07/careers/payday-lj-salary-survey-2014/

Glenville State College (2016). Earn a Free College Degree. [Flyer]. Glenville, West Virginia: Glenville State College.

Ingraham, C. (2015, January 6). The U.S. has more jails than colleges. Here's a map of where those prisoners live. Retrieved from https://www.washingtonpost.com/news/wonk/wp/2015/01/06/the-u-s-has-more-jails-than-colleges-heres-a-map-of-where-those-prisoners-live/

Institute of Museum and Library Services: State Allotments. (2015, July 07). Retrieved from https://www.imls.gov/grants/grants-state/state-allotments

Lewis, Director, Arizona Department of Corrections, et al. v. Casey et al., (1996). (n.d.). Retrieved November 14, 2016, from http://caselaw.findlaw.com/us-supreme-court/518/343.html

Number Employed in Libraries. (2015, April). Retrieved from http://www.ala.org/tools/libfactsheets/alalibraryfactsheet02

Prison Libraries. (n.d.). Retrieved November 15, 2016, from https://www.cde.state.co.us/cdelib/prisonlibraries/index

Rand Corporation, Office of Media Relations. (2013, August 22). Education and Vocational Training in Prisons Reduces Recidivism, Improves Job Outlook [Press release]. Retrieved from http://www.rand.org/news/press/2013/08/22.html

Steeves, H. (2010, August 10). Prison librarian testifies on attack in case against inmate. Retrieved from http://bangordailynews.com/2010/08/10/news/prison-librarian-testifies-on-attack-in-case-against-inmate/

United States Department of Education, Press Office. (2016, June 24). Http://www.ed.gov/news/press-releases/12000-incarcerated-students-enroll-postsecondary-educational-and-training-programs-through-education-departments-new-second-chance-pell-pilot-program

[Press release]. Retrieved from http://www.ed.gov/news/press-releases/12000-incarcerated-students-enroll-postsecondary-educational-and-training-programs-through-education-departments-new-second-chance-pell-pilot-program

Wexler, E. (2016, June 24). U.S. expands Pell Grant program to 12,000 in prison. Retrieved from https://www.insidehighered.com/news/2016/06/24/us-expands-pell-grant-program-12000-prison

## THE REMIX: HIP HOP INFORMATION LITERACY PEDAGOGY IN THE 21ST CENTURY

(ACRL), A. (2015-2016). Assessment in Action, Lincoln University: Institutional Profile. U.S. National Center for Education Statistics. Retrieved December 1, 2016, from https://apply.ala.org/aia/docs/institution_profile/13748#institution_info

ACRL, B. (2016, January 11). Framework for Information Literacy for Higher Education. Retrieved December 1, 2016, from Association of College and Research Libraries: http://www.ala.org/acrl/standards/ilframework

Bain, K. (2004). What Do They Do When They Teach. In What the Best College Teachers Do (pp. 18-18). Massachusetts, United States: Harvard University Press.

Hip hop quotes. Retrieved December 8, 2016, from Hip Hop Quotes | Quotes from various hip-hop songs., http://hip-hop-quotes.tumblr.com/

Quotes About Hip Hop (76 quotes). (n.d.). Retrieved December 08, 2016, from http://www.goodreads.com/quotes/tag/hip-hop. Header quotes retrieved from this site.

Walker, D. (2008). Report on Information Literacy and the Mic: Teaching Higher Education Students Critical Research Skills Using Hip Hop Lyricism. McNair Scholars Research Journal, 1(1, Article 4). Retrieved from http://commons.emich.edu/mcnair/vol1/iss1/4/

## USING TECHNOLOGY TO COMMUNICATE, EDUCATE AND EMPOWER GIRLS OF COLOR (GOC)

A. (2016). About. Retrieved August 29, 2016, from http://www.latinagirlscode.org/about/

Ashcraft, C., Eger, E., & Friend, M. (2012). Girls in It: The facts (Rep.). Retrieved November 20, 2016, from National Center for Women and Information Technology website: https://www.ncwit.org/sites/default/files/resources/girlsinit_thefacts_fullreport2012.pdf

Committee, A. C. (2016). ALSC Blog. Retrieved August 29, 2016, from http://www.alsc.ala.org/blog/

Global Libraries. (1999). Retrieved August 29, 2016, from http://www.gatesfoundation.org/What-We-Do/Global-Development/Global-Libraries

Johnston, M. P. (2012). School Librarians as Technology Integration Leaders: Enablers and Barriers to Leadership Enactment. School Library Research, 1-33. American Association of School Librarians. Retrieved August 29, 2016 from http://www.ala.org/aasl/slr/volume15/johnston

Lopez, M., Caspe, M., & McWilliams, L. (2016). Public Libraries: A Vital Space for Family Engagement. Retrieved August 29, 2016, from http://www.hfrp.org/publications-resources/browse-our-publications/public-libraries-a-vital-space-for-family-engagement

Mack, C. (2015, August 5). 3-2-1 IMPACT! Inclusive and Impactful Teen Services [Web log post]. Retrieved August 29, 2016, from http://yalsa.ala.org/blog/2015/08/05/3-2-1-impact-inclusive-and-impactful-teen-services/

Resource guide. (2016). Retrieved August 29, 2016, from http://wikis.ala.org/yalsa/index.php/Resource_guide

Remarks to Multi-Stakeholder Forum on Science, Technology and Innovation for the Sustainable Development Goals Secretary-General Ban Ki-moon. (2016). Retrieved August 29, 2016, from https://www.un.org/sg/en/content/sg/speeches/2016-06-06/remarks-multi-stakeholder-forum-science-technology-and-innovation

United Nations. (2016) Transforming our world: The 2030

Agenda for Sustainable Development in Sustainable Development Knowledge Platform. Retrieved February 25, 2017, from https://sustainabledevelopment.un.org/post2015/transformingourworld

What We Do. (2016). Retrieved August 29, 2016, from http://www.gatesfoundation.org/What-We-Do

What We Do. (2016). Retrieved August 29, 2016, from http://www.blackgirlscode.com/what-we-do.html

## LOWRIDERS IN SPACE: HOW A GRAPHIC NOVEL BUILT A COMMUNITY

Author Note: When I wrote Lowriders in Space, I didn't keep track of the references I used, so I'm including sources that share the type of information that encouraged me to write the book, as well as resources I mention in the article.

2016-2017 TBA Master List Resources. (2015, September 26). Retrieved October 23, 2016, from Texas Bluebonnet Award Program Committee website: https://texasbluebonnetaward2017.wordpress.com/

Aesop Prizes and Aesop Accolades. (n.d.). Retrieved November 7, 2016, from American Folklore Society website: http://www.afsnet.org/?Aesop

Macias, M. (2015, September 25). Lowriders in Space (Book Review) [Web log post]. Retrieved from Lowrider Librarian: http://lowriderlibrarian.blogspot.com/2015/02/lowriders-in-space-book-review.html

Profile American Facts for Features Hispanic Heritage Month 2011: Sept. 15 - Oct. 15. (2011, August 26). Retrieved September 25, 2016, from United States Census Bureau website: https://www.census.gov/newsroom/releases/archives/facts_for_features_special_editions/cb11-ff18.html

Saulny, S. (2011, March 24). Census Data Presents Rise in Multiracial Population of Youths. New York Times. Retrieved from http://www.nytimes.com/2011/03/25/us/25race.html?_r=0

We Need Diverse Books. (n.d.). Retrieved September 25, 2016, from http://weneeddiversebooks.org/

White, M. (2012, July 28). Why boys' literacy skills lag behind girls' and how to bridge the reading gap. Retrieved September 25, 2016, from Deseret News Utah website: http://www.deseretnews.com/article/765592913/Many-working-to-bridge-wide-gender-reading-gap-in-the-US.html?pg=all

gonadotrophins that are excreted in quantity by pregnant women only. These tests were extremely reliable, but slow, and a year later it was found that tests on rabbits could be completed in a day or two.
Then in 1931 there came a breakthrough. A scientist working in Cape Town found that urine of pregnant women injected into a female clawed frog would cause it to discharge its eggs 5–18 hours later. Here was a test that was not only twice as quick as any other, but it left the animal alive. Each frog could be used many times, so the process of confirming pregnancy became rapid and reliable and, consequently, clawed frogs were exported all over the world.
Pregnancy testing
The first test for confirming pregnancy at an early stage was devised in 1928. Samples of urine were injected into mice, which were killed and examined 5 days later. If the urine came from a pregnant woman, changes would be found in the ovaries of the mouse, caused by substances called
E Elkan, NHPA

figure 12

# Index

CPSIA information can be obtained
at www.ICGtesting.com
Printed in the USA
LVHW081918300819
629535LV00016B/392/P